THE STORY OF
THE SPORTING GUN

Glass engraving by Gernod Schluiffer, Kitzbühl, Austria

THE STORY OF
THE SPORTING GUN

PAINTINGS BY ANDREW ELLIS
WRITTEN BY RANULF RAYNER

David & Charles

This book is dedicated in memory of my father, a great countryman, and to my eldest son Ralph who at the age of eleven shot his first driven pheasant – with an air rifle

A contribution from the proceeds of this book will be given to CIC (Conseil International de la Chasse)

A DAVID & CHARLES BOOK

First published in the UK in 1991
First paperback edition 2003

Copyright © Ranulf Rayner, 1991, 2003

Distributed in North America
by F&W Publications, Inc.
4700 East Galbraith Road
Cincinnati, OH 45236
1-800-289-0963

A catalogue record for this book is available from the British Library.

ISBN 0 7153 1574 9
Printed in Singapore   by KHL Printing
for David & Charles
Brunel House   Newton Abbot   Devon

Visit our website at www.davidandcharles.co.uk

David & Charles books are available from all good bookshops; alternatively you can contact our Orderline on (0)1626 334555 or write to us at FREEPOST EX2110, David & Charles Direct, Newton Abbot, TQ12 4ZZ (no stamp required UK mainland).

Uniform with this book, and by the same author

The Paintings of the America's Cup
Paintings by Tim Thompson

The Story of Yachting
Paintings by Tim Thompson

The Story of Skiing
Paintings by Robert Guy

DAVID & CHARLES'
FIELDSPORTS AND FISHING TITLES

The Angling Times Book of Coarse Fishing
  Allan Haines and Mac Campbell
Big Fish from Famous Waters
  Compiled by Chris Turnbull
Catching Big Tench   Len Arbery
The Complete Book of Float Fishing   Allan Haines
The Complete Gundog
  Compiled by John Humphreys
The Countrysportsman's Record Book &
  Journal   John Humphreys
Cultivating a Shoot   J. C. Jeremy Hobson
The Fields in Winter Sporting Memories of a
  Bygone Age   Graham Downing
The Glorious Grouse   Brian P. Martin
The Great Anglers   John Bailey
The Great Hunts Foxhunting Countries of the
  World   Alastair Jackson
The Great Salmon Beats   Crawford Little
The Great Shoots Britain's Premier Sporting
  Estates   Brian P. Martin
Hunting An Introductory Handbook
  R. W. F. Poole
Purdey's: The Guns and the Family
  Richard Beaumont
Shooting Pigeons John Humphreys
Sporting Birds of the British Isles   Brian P. Martin
Success with Salmon   Crawford Little
Success with Trout   John Dawson, Martin
  Cairncross and Chris Ogborne
Tales of the Old Gamekeepers   Brian P. Martin
What Every Gun Should Know
  J. C. Jeremy Hobson

George Augustus, Earl of Belfast (1769–1844) – Gainsborough

CONTENTS

Shooter and loader changing guns—Position No. 1.

Shooter and loader changing guns—Position No. 2.

Shooter and loader changing guns—Position No. 3.

Duck shooting in winter – Strodamus, circa 1570

FOREWORD

Unpalatable as it may seem to those who are opposed to field sports – or blood sports as they have chosen to call them – the fact remains that much of the countryside that we care for in the British Isles today is the result of the evolution of those sports. Many of our parks and woodland coverts were originally planted or adapted to harbour game. A not insignificant part in this evolution has been played by game shooting and the advent of the breech loading shotgun in the second half of the last century.

Shooting men who had hitherto walked up and shot a relatively small number of birds over dogs would now, because of the speed of loading, enjoy the far more exciting sport of shooting driven game. As a result, the heather-clad uplands of Scotland and the North of England became the Mecca of shooting men who came from all over the world to enjoy the new and special sport of shooting driven grouse. This brought great benefits, especially financial, to some of the most remote and impoverished areas of Britain. Similarly, in the lowlands of Britain, new coverts were planted and old woodlands were rehabilitated for the new sport of driving pheasants. Today these shooting coverts are an important and valued feature of our countryside, of benefit both to game and wildlife. All of us who are involved in shooting know that good game conservation is synonymous with good wildlife conservation.

However, it is not only the rural environment that has benefited from the evolution of shooting. The economy of the countryside, especially in earlier times, was a beneficiary also. The numbers of game-keepers swelled with the burgeoning interest in shooting, and farm and estate workers earned extra money as beaters on shooting days. Local tradesmen gained from the great shooting parties of earlier years, just as they did later from syndicate shoots, and do latterly from the commercially let shooting days which are an important feature of today's shooting scene. The same process has taken place in some of the less favoured agricultural areas of Spain, where commercial partridge shoots have brought huge benefits to some of the very poor villages. Yet Spain still has the finest reservoir of wildlife in Western Europe, and that is more than can be said of some other Mediterranean countries where the traditions of managed shooting, with appropriate legislation to support it, does not exist.

Another beneficiary of shooting has been the British gun trade. Just as at the beginning of the last century the ownership of a Joseph Manton gun was the ambition of all shooting men, so today's sports-men from all over the world still regard the 'best' English shotgun as the epitome of the art of gun making. For a fine gun is indeed a work of art, and anyone who doubts that should visit the Royal Armories at the Tower of London and see some of the beautiful guns in our National Museums of Arms and Armour. Moreover, like all works of art, fine guns are a good investment although I feel that this aspect of gun ownership was rather overdone by an American who I met several years ago. I admired a very fine gold-encrusted Purdey gun which he was holding, and his comment was 'That beat-up old thing! Why, I have thirty better pairs of Purdeys in my cellar at home.' I had to remark that I thought that cellars were better suited to the storage of another good investment – good wine!

I cannot close my foreword without remarking on the beautiful illustrations of the young artist, Andrew Ellis, who depicts the shooting scene so well. They worthily complement a book which will be enjoyed by shooting men and fine gun enthusiasts alike.

THE DUKE OF WELLINGTON, 1990

Self portrait by Ben Marshall, the eighteenth-century sporting artist

INTRODUCTION

BANG-G-G-G! The sound of the shot sang in my ears as the blood welled into my cheeks. My father shouted from the end of the breakfast room table, 'Put down that gun', and my mother fell out of her chair. Around her the splintered and smoking floorboards were evidence of how close she had been to death – and the bunch of rabbits I had ceremoniously carried in through the French windows seemed suddenly to be of no consequence at all.

I did not get back my treasured .410 for more than two years by which time I already had my eye on my father's pair of Greeners, for, regretting that he had once shot too many tigers in India, he was already contemplating retirement from the chase. The old folding poacher's gun with its hammer action had always been notoriously difficult to uncock, particularly when the hammers were wet or covered in oil but, as I had later explained to my mother, at least I had remembered one golden rule that frosty morning – to keep the weapon pointed at the floor.

Hammer guns are cause for much nostalgia and some big shots still swear by them. I know of one enthusiast who, fanning his hammers like Billy the Kid, was able to shoot four clay pigeons in the air together. We were all demonstrating our prowess at clay pigeon shooting on one occasion when my mother, who was out exercising her Pekinese dog and oblivious to what was going on, walked right into the line of fire – narrowly missing death by the 'bullet' for a second time. Surprisingly, in the early days of the flintlock, bullets or solid shot were actually used for shooting at game birds, but at first, due to the painfully slow ignition of the powder, hitting them was quite a different matter. Only when a method was devised for speeding up the burning process, described later in this book, did the shotgun come into its own, all major modifications being complete soon after the turn of the twentieth century.

It is interesting to consider, in these times of 'progress', how little the design of the shotgun has altered over the past years. Indeed, as is often the case, it is not so much the equipment but rather the sport that has changed. The fitting of a bespoke fowling piece by an aproned craftsman in an oil soaked gunshop thankfully just continues, but here any similarities with shooting 'before the war' end. For, having acquired a gun licence and a bag of cartridges, whose colour often no longer indicates the bore, the next step is to show the colour of your money if you want any decent sport at all. Gone are most of those friendly 'boundary days' and the rough shoots that brought men a little closer to nature; here to stay are the hundreds of bird days or the hundreds of brace days that make or break relations with the owner or the gamekeeper – shooting's newly promoted managing director.

Efficient game management has never been more important than in our now overcrowded society – but it is still much misunderstood. To many objectors the licensed shooting of big game in Kenya was outrageous at the time, and yet the recent slaughter of the African elephant must be attributed largely to those objectors themselves. Culling the old, infirm or imperfect animals not only benefited reproduction of the stock in later years, but, more importantly, the sale of expensive hunting licences helped pay the wages of professional game wardens to look after the animals. No game wardens – no game, for a greed-smitten specimen of *Homo Sapiens*, which should have been culled long ago, soon made sure of that. As night follows day, the same fate awaits all game denied the misquoted 'luxury' of a human keeper. My book rates game management and keepering highly, and it traces the development of that profession not only in relation to the sporting world today, but to the restoration and conservation of the wild as we once knew it, and would like to know it again tomorrow.

Since the first half of the nineteenth century game bird shooting, surprisingly, has been largely neglected by artists. Due in part to the growing popularity of photography during the sport's most formative years (1865–1914), and in part to the initial dislike for the sport of driving game birds (which was introduced over the same period), the idea of including a line of 'Guns' in any painting was generally considered unacceptable. With the demise of the great shooting parties of the Edwardian era also died much of the enthusiasm for commissioning shooting art, and it is hardly surprising that as a consequence of two world wars and a changed shooting public, the market has been slow to return. Among the new generation of sporting artists, however, Andrew Ellis is already making his mark, and his work is a fine example of the contemporary 'art of shooting', which is now, at last, enjoying a sustained recovery.

'Birds of a feather' may 'flock together', but most varieties of game birds, as illustrated by brush and pen so cleverly in this book, have such widely differing habits that they should be noted by all who pursue them. However, many of today's 'Guns', as they assemble for a shoot, will have no such thoughts on their minds. Forgotten are the skills of the gamekeeper, the careful propagation of birds and cover, and the long wet nights spent waiting up for a fox. Today a sizeable bag and a good shooting lunch are usually the only criteria that matter. Commercialism has changed the face of sport everywhere and, like many activities that are gaining in popularity, shooting is in equal danger of losing its sporting reputation. It is therefore up to us, as sportsmen, to control the excesses before others control them for us, to learn more about the vanishing craft of shooting as practised in the past, and to write the next chapter of *The Story of the Sporting Gun* together.

EVOLUTION OF THE SHOTGUN

The wheel-lock, first invented at Nuremberg, Germany, in 1515

They should be put in flat side upwards, stand well clear of the hammer, and yet be long enough to throw it. Screw them in with leather; as lead strains the cock, and cloth is dangerous, from being liable to catch fire.

Preparation of the flintlock
COLONEL PETER HAWKER, 1821

In tracing today's hammerless ejector from the invention of the first matchlock rifle in the early part of the fifteenth century, it is interesting to consider the military significance of firearms at that time. 'Those abominable bullets', wrote a celebrated French general, 'which had been discharged by cowardly and base knaves, who would never have dared meet true soldiers face to face, were clearly from one of those artifices only the devil employs.' Though effective at 200yd (183m), however, for

Manton's flint-lock muzzleloader, early nineteenth century

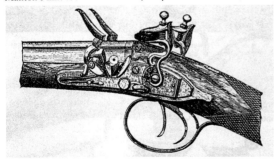

Powder flasks

more than a hundred years weapons remained so inaccurate that it was calculated, more often than not, that a soldier had to fire away his own weight in lead for every man he killed.

Guns designed for sporting purposes were also introduced during the fifteenth century, but principally in Italy, Spain and Germany and to a lesser extent in France. In Great Britain little use was made of them for shooting game until the latter half of the seventeenth century, when most of the guns continued to be of foreign make. The evolution of the shotgun from that time can best be divided into eight successive stages.

The first stage, the matchlock gun, had the crudest form of ignition. To fire the weapon, the sportsman first blew on the end of his fuse, then slid open the cover of the priming pan, and a pressure from the trigger plunged a glowing match into the loose powder, which, if he was lucky, was dry enough to ignite the main charge through a touch-hole. There was, inevitably, an unpredictable delay before any lead left the barrel, particularly if it was raining, and the target would meanwhile run or fly to safety.

The second stage, the wheel-lock gun, which was in use by the end of the sixteenth century, had a steel wheel that, when wound up and released, revolved at high speed against a pyrites stone, sending a shower of sparks into the centre of the priming powder. The discharge was almost instantaneous, quicker indeed than the flintlock action that followed it, but although it made bird shooting possible for the first time, the simplicity of the latter soon caused the wheel-lock to go out of fashion.

By 1700 most sportsmen were armed with flintlock fowling pieces. The early flintlocks were very well made but usually single barrelled with a barrel length of about 44in (112cm). The favourite calibre was 20-bore, and although some double-barrelled guns were also produced at the time, they were of over and under design with the barrels being revolved by hand on a pivot. A well chosen flint would last for 20 or 30 shots without being touched and the action was so straightforward that flintlock guns, culminating in the advent of the double-barrelled side-by-side sporting gun, invented by Joseph Manton early in the nineteenth century, retained their popularity for almost 200 years.

In 1807, a Scottish minister, the Rev Alexander Forsyth, somewhat suprisingly took out a patent for firing weapons with a compound of fulminate of mercury. A magazine was to be screwed into the breech end of the barrel so that a small quantity of the compound came under a percussion hammer every time the magazine was revolved by hand. This invention, known as the detonating system, marked the fourth stage in the development of the sporting gun. During the following year a Genevan gun maker named Pauly, then practising in Paris, manufactured the first advanced prototype. On pulling the trigger, a needle pierced a cap, which then ignited the charge. It was from this gun that the famous Lefaucheux breech-loader was later developed.

The detonating gun revolutionised the world of firearms, but at first the caps were so badly made that they often shattered, sometimes scarring sportsmen for life. 'Moreover', stated the redoubtable Colonel Hawker', the sudden and additional recoil of a detonator is apt – if the shooter be not careful – to strike the hand back and give him a severe blow on the nose'. Such sentiments were soon to result in many modifications and improvements of the original design. Most notable of these was the tube-lock, perfected in 1818, again by the now master gun maker, Joseph Manton. The tube-lock, which marked the fifth stage, only differed from the percussion cap in that a small copper tube containing fulminate of mercury was inserted into the touch-hole. More reliable than its predecessor, it also held a greater

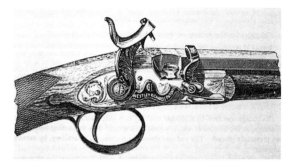

The Westley-Richards detonating gun, 1821

amount of compound and was less affected by wet weather.

Compared with the flintlock, however, the detonating gun had a relatively short life. Within forty years it was already being superseded by the sixth stage in the evolution of the shotgun, the pin-fire breech-loader. A simple method of breech-loading had been tried out by Robert, a Parisian gun maker, early in the nineteenth century. By pulling a lever, a hinged breech-block could be raised in order to insert the shot and the charge. Early breech-loaders were designed to be primed either by powder, pellet, paper cap or copper tube, but later on the copper cap was found to be superior to all of them, although many sportsmen still remained sceptical about the whole idea. The French Lefaucheux breech-loader, manufactured in 1836, was one of the first guns to fire a crude form of cartridge and the more advanced cartridge case with its own copper cap, named the pin-fire cartridge, was simply a logical development.

The Lefaucheux breech-loader, 1836

The Original Lefaucheux Breech-loader : 1836.

English gun makers quickly jumped on the band-wagon and although Joseph Manton had died in 1835 leaving the industry, as Hawker put it, 'like frogs without a King', a growing number of now famous names, such as the first James Purdey, once Manton's employee, engaged themselves in bettering each other's techniques. The development of the hammerless gun, the seventh stage, had been retarded by the ultimate popularity of the pin-fire gun, which was based on different principles, but in 1871 an Englishman, T. Murcott, produced the first hammer-less gun to be acceptable in the field. (The writer is conscious that this is only a cursory summary of the evolution of the shotgun. Over the period iron barrels had given way to steel, and there had been such a proliferation of inventions that he felt it preferable to concentrate on the principal ones only.)

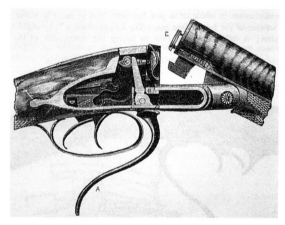

Murcott's hammerless gun, 1871

The eighth and final chapter was also to be written by an Englishman, J. Needham, barely three years later. By using the mainspring of the lock to provide the necessary force, Needham was the first person to introduce independent extractors for each barrel, resulting in the expended cartridge only being thrown clear.

Thus the nineteenth century saw the complete evolution of the double-barrelled sporting gun from the flintlock to the hammerless ejector as we still know it today.

THE CARTRIDGE

The Needham ejector gun, 1874

The pin-fire cartridge was not the result of one great invention, but rather of man's general endeavour to provide a practical answer to the problems associated with the muzzle-loader.

With the advent of the breech-loading musket, it became obvious that the charge behind the ball needed to be contained. 'The immense escape of explosive matter past the ball prevented the possibility of any velocity worthy of the name,' complained Greener at the time. But early attempts at cartridge making were equally unsuccessful, largely because it had not been realised that the barrel actually expands at the moment of firing. Only when this was acknowledged, and cartridge cases made of thinner material, was the problem solved. The force of the explosion was now used to expand the cartridge case, thus sealing the breech and driving the shot forward. No better method of firing a shotgun has been devised since.

From the time that expanding cartridges were first used in the 1830s, modifications have been primarily concerned with the method of detonation. The pin-fire method was prone to gases escaping from the pin-hole in the breech, and the cartridges, with their projecting pins (see drawing of the Lefaucheux breech-loader), were difficult to carry. This led to the development of the central-fire cartridge, which, once given a rim so that it could be extracted, has changed little in design since its introduction in the 1850s. It is remarkable that black powder, with all its obscuring smoke, was the universal charge up until this period, when 'wood', or 'white', powder was discovered by a Colonel Schultze. Since then, with the development of numerous nitro-compounds, the manufacture of sporting cartridges has steadily improved. Brass cartridge cases have given way to paper cases and they in turn have given way to waterproof plastic cases. Paper wadding has been superseded by plastic wadding and lead shot, in environmentally sensitive areas, to steel shot. But more about that later.

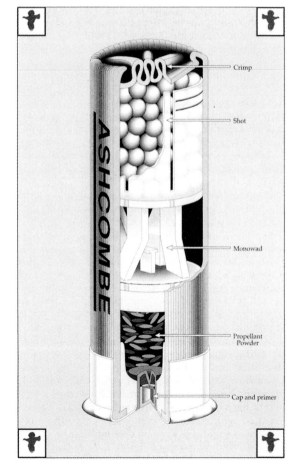

ASHCOMBE

Crimp

Shot

Monowad

Propellant Powder

Cap and primer

A modern cartridge: some manufacturers unfortunately no longer keep to the colour code denoting calibre, which may cause a 12-bore cartridge to be inadvertently loaded when, for instance, a 16-bore cartridge is already up the breach

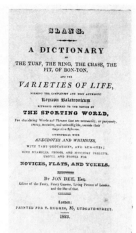

The art of shooting flying – poster, early nineteenth century

GAME SHOOTING

If, during the fifteenth century, it had been necessary for a soldier to carry his own weight in lead in order to kill just one man, consider how much lead a sportsman would have had to carry to shoot a bird in flight. However, during the reign of Henry VIII (1509–1547) the English parliament passed several acts regulating the use of 'cross-bows and hand guns for hunting game', and in 1609 a Giacomo Franco published an illustration of shooting birds on the wing – proving that the sport existed then. 'We can scarcely imagine that any sportsman can aspire to shoot flying game with an arquebuse', a writer stated a hundred years later, but by the eighteenth century books were already being produced on 'Shooting Flying'.

At this point it is worth considering a few of the difficulties of handling the old muzzle-loaders:

'A frequent and ever present danger', quotes W. W. Greener in his classic book *The Gun and its Development*, 'was that of accidental discharge while loading. Then again there was the risk of overloading, for it was no uncommon thing for the sportsman to put both charges of powder into the same barrel, sometimes with disastrous consequences.

'Ramming down the charge often carried with it damp fouling, naturally giving way to indifferent and irregular results. The ramrod was a constant worry, frequently breaking, and at times, when the occasion arose for a rapid shot, it would be left in the barrel and fired from it by an excited sportsman.'

Difficulties in cleaning it were no better:

'The cleaning of the barrels was a troublesome and dirty job', Greener continues, 'it was frequently necessary to scour them out with boiling water, and the breeches soon became so fouled and rusted that the only way a gun maker could manage to repair them was to pour oil down the barrel while holding it over a fire. Some nasty accidents occurred when doing this, through omitting to properly withdraw the charge.'

Yet it seems incredible that Greener's father, in his book *Gunnery* in 1858, wrote about the new breech-loader: 'Notwithstanding all the skill and ingenuity brought to bear upon it, it is, we think, sufficient to prove that breech-loading guns cannot be made sufficiently durable to yield any reasonable return for the extra expense and trouble attending their fabrication.' (A possible explanation is that he may not have been fully aware at the time he wrote the book of the new central-fire cartridge which led to modifications of the gun.)

W. W. Greener was a gun maker who did not stand still. Given the second name of Wellington after *The Gun*, written by his father in 1834, had been dedicated to the Duke, he was constantly patenting new actions. His guns became so popular throughout the world that armed outriders, hired to escort important personages, came to be known as 'Greeners'. But other gun makers were similarly active, and in England by the second half of the nineteenth century a substantial choice of weaponry was being offered to the shooting public.

Although on the Continent prodigious bags of game were already being shot, in England, until this time, such massacres were considered hardly sportsmanlike. Far more important were legends, often told around the fireside, of men such as Sir Francis Chantry, who, although blind in one eye, on 20 November 1829 at Holkham in Norfolk, killed two woodcock with one shot, later immortalising the feat by carving the birds in marble. Another legendary figure, the redoubtable Colonel Peter Hawker, who died in 1853, was not only the most famous British shot of his age, but has probably been talked about more than any marksman before or since. The colonel knew how a gun should be made, from lock to stock, from the bend of a dolphin-cock to the reboring of a pitted barrel. Once, with his trusty flintlock, he was credited with shooting seventy-seven partridges out of seventy-eight. He scarcely ever missed and was as efficient with a muzzle-loader as those who fancied themselves with breech-loaders were later on. But

Above: Chantry's famous shot   *Below*: Colonel Peter Hawker

Walsingham

Sepr. 18. 88.

above all he was as staunch a conservative as most of the sportsmen who have followed him, each in turn showing the same doubt and dislike for innovation and improvement.

One theory about those marksmen of yesteryear was that the game was tamer and the countryside wilder than today, affording better opportunities for both man and dog. But the truth is that most shooting stories since then have not been so much about the traditional walking up of game or of the stealth and cunning needed to bag them, but more often about vast numbers of driven birds – a previously inconceivable thought – that might now be shot to a single gun or on a single day. In 1888, for instance, the celebrated Victorian sportsman, Lord Walsingham, who was determined to enhance his already impressive reputation, had so many grouse driven past his lone butt, that he shot no less than 1,070 birds in seven hours! Today such exhibitionism would, thank heavens, be considered pointless, but at that time hunting, shooting and fishing were important symbols of the outdoor life which the English gentry, as a class, were regarding increasingly as the only proper

way to exist. During the Edwardian era that followed it was not uncommon for a gunner to blaze off as many as 15,000 cartridges over the winter season, resulting in some astonishing records.

World War I had an immediate impact on game shooting, most British gun makers, such as Purdey's, turning their attentions to helping in the war effort. It was hardly surprising, therefore, that the sport did not really recover until the mid-1920s to early 1930s. But although this was hailed as the second golden period in the sport's history, brilliant shots such as George Philippi and his wife establishing impressive reputations, the world of the sporting Gun was already changing dramatically. In November 1936 *The Field* published the following obituary: 'The day of the great shots, or at any rate, of the great "professional" shots is over. No longer is it possible, except to the very favoured few, to pass the time from the beginning of August to after the New Year in one country house after another, moving from moor to moor, or from manor to manor.' Hastened by the outbreak of World War II in Europe, life in the shooting field was never to be quite the same again.

Above: King Edward VII in action   *Below*: King George V shooting

GAME MANAGEMENT

Game management may be described as the art of making land produce sustained annual crops of game for recreational purposes. Without such management many species of game and much of our beautiful countryside, certainly in Great Britain, would already have disappeared.

The concept of game management dates back to biblical times. Moses decreed: 'If a bird's nest chance to be before thee in any way – thou shalt not take the dam with the young', (Deuteronomy 22:6), implying that the dam should be left for breeding purposes. Much later Marco Polo describes the game laws of Kublai, 'The Great Khan' (AD 1259–1294): 'There is an order which prohibits every person throughout all the countries subject to the Great Khan from daring to kill any large birds between the months of March and October.'

History has shown that game management probably began with restrictions on hunting. Other measures followed – a likely sequence of events being:

1 Hunting controls
2 Predator controls
3 Land reservation
4 Game restocking
5 Environmental controls

In England written laws establishing closed seasons go back to King Henry VIII (1509–1547), who decreed that waterfowl and their eggs should be protected from 31 May to 31 August each year, partridges and pheasants being included later by James I (1603–1625). Restrictive laws in America were first introduced in pre-Revolutionary times and hunting controls increased through the 1800s as the game decreased in numbers.

In the 1200s Frederick II, Holy Roman Emperor, is believed to have been the first to have organised predator control as we know it today. Hoping to improve his favourite sport of falconry, as recorded in his book *De Artibus Vernandi*, he set about conserving the game population on a scale that would impress any modern gamekeeper. Public bounties, as a means of controlling predators, were introduced in England by Henry VIII in 1520.

By the fifteenth century, although there were a large number of English hunting reservations, first granted by Canute the Dane's 'Charter of the Forest'

in 1062, they remained prey for poachers. But in 1495 Henry VII passed a law forbidding the taking of pheasants and partridges on other people's land, thus drafting the first laws of trespass. Not until the twentieth century were fully protected game reserves, such as the national parks in Canada and the United States, established.

Restocking with pheasants was certainly practised in England as early as 1523 and with mallard duck by 1631. In Bohemia pheasants were being artificially raised by 1598. But pheasants were not introduced to the United States much before 1900, since when the population has been maintained largely by state game farms.

However, only recently has the world woken up to the fifth and most important stage of game management: the care of our vanishing countryside and the conservation of the hunting environment as a whole (considered later in this book). Great Britain is already leading the way in implementing far-reaching countryside codes and appropriate legislation, but hunters in general, and those that enjoy game bird shooting in particular, now have the most important role to play in ensuring the continuance of the sport of 'shooting flying'.

The managed shoot

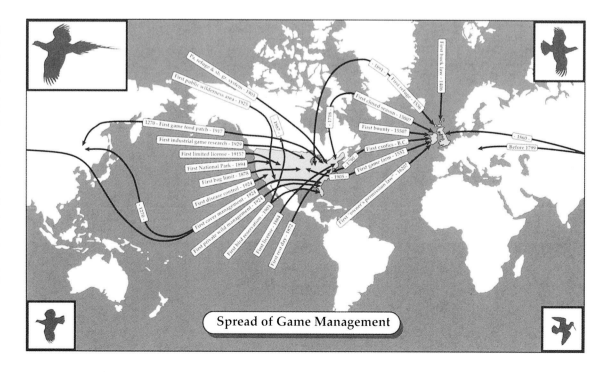

Spread of Game Management

BEGINNER'S LUCK

If a person is extremely nervous from hearing the report of his gun, or from the noise of the rising game, let him prime his ears with cotton, and his inside with tincture of bark and sal volatile.

Instructions to Young Sportsmen
COLONEL PETER HAWKER

There are few better ways of learning to shoot than stalking rabbits or pigeons with a little .410.

Everyone remembers his first gun; it may have marked one of his life's most important milestones – the moment of responsibility. If handled carefully it does not lead to the moment of truth, but all too often there is a tragedy, and later in life accidents in the shooting field may often be attributed to poor instruction at an early age, or sometimes to no instruction whatsoever.

Old shooting signals, circa 1850

'On my first tremendous occasion out shooting I bombarded the old keeper with questions about kicking, but he refused to commit himself by saying that guns did not kick at all. I had gathered from other sources that it was no worse than having a tooth out – "Of course, it may hurt just a little, but it's over directly" – but when I pulled the trigger it knocked me over, and I found my double–barrelled gun pointing directly at him. Needless to say I got a pasting, I suppose you'd call it beginner's luck!'

Jim Vestey

Traditionally country gentlemen's sons were often taught to shoot by the head gamekeeper. But today most young shots seldom have that opportunity, and modern gamekeepers, unlike many of their sometimes

16

ruffianly predecessors, are so busy tending their flocks of birds, that they have little time for giving instruction, let alone teaching a few lessons to the ever-attentive vermin. The first sensible step is more likely, therefore, to be a visit to a shooting school, where a high standard of instruction is guaranteed. Fathers, although they may try hard, are not so likely to be listened to.

At shooting school the top priority is to make certain that a boy's gun fits correctly. From the time that a boy begins to shoot to the time he stops growing, the essential limb measurements are unlikely to alter so dramatically that the gun will not still fit him when he is grown up. Then, when the time comes to change the gun, the correct weapon may be chosen almost instinctively. Young pupils at shooting school are inclined to suffer from overeagerness, and self control is one of the prerequisites for becoming a good shot. The rest of the instruction, on stance, balance and follow through, will either flow naturally or require some extremely hard work.

If the wind is right and the going soft, it is often possible to get quite close to a rabbit. But at the moment of self congratulation the rabbit may stop nibbling and sit bolt upright – then the opportunity to bag him most likely is lost

THE ROUGH SHOOT

A rough lot!

Rough shooting has not only been the start of most formal shoots but the finish of many formal shots – for 'rough' means walking! However, those who prefer to sit on shooting sticks, waiting for the birds to be driven past them, are but a small minority of the shooting public, and luckily, whether they are prepared to walk or not, hidden in the clouds of cigar smoke there is one admirable spin-off – the sport of rough shooting itself.

Such is the pressure on the countryside that without organised shooting and organised keeping the game bird population would face near extinction and the rough shoot would probably cease to exist. Not that rough shooting is entirely about shooting game birds, it also concerns hares and rabbits, pigeon and duck and in general the pursuit of every bird or small mammal that can find a useful place in a country larder.

Most rough shoots are run as syndicates, one member of which may act as the gamekeeper. A number of birds may be released into the wild in the usual way or, more likely, the shoot will rely on the bulk of its stock flying in conveniently from some of its more prosperous neighbours. The stock will usually be so precious that great trouble is taken in feeding the birds, sometimes by more than one member of the syndicate, and the shoot's boundaries are likely to be jealously patrolled. Vermin, particularly, are given little quarter, and 'Charlie', as the fox may endearingly be called, is far more likely to have that 'smile wiped off his face' by a rough shooting lot than by any of the posher 'Guns' next door. Jays, crows and magpies also tend to have a much harder time, for on driven days Guns tend to concentrate on game not vermin, and no shooting is allowed between drives. A rough shoot may well be the ultimate place in which it is possible to find a wild pheasant, and because a wild hen is at least four times as productive as its hand-reared counterpart, each may be worth more than its weight in gold.

In the days when only rough shooting was available, Colonel Peter Hawker, the greatest shot of his generation, would spend hours outmanoeuvring a single old cock pheasant. 'When a man is no further versed in shooting than to have become quite expert at bringing down his bird, he has only learnt about one-third of the art. Knowing where to place himself for shots – how to spring the game to advantage – what days and weather to choose for the different kinds of sport – constitute at least the other two-thirds,' he wrote.

The rough shoot provides the ideal environment for any beginner; there is no better way of discovering the countryside and all its interesting ways. Often it costs nothing except dedication to be a member of a rough shoot, particularly in an area were there are plenty of wild birds, and the rewards are plentiful. By nature man is a predator, although his senses are greatly deficient in both hearing and smell, and to stalk prey which are blessed with so many natural advantages is a challenge that any young man will find hard to equal, certainly in the concrete world we now live in.

Opposite: The rough shoot

The smart lot

18

WALKING UP PHEASANTS

pheasant, is given by Aristophanes of Byzantium (c180BC), who described it as a domestic bird kept by wealthy families. Later, in the fourth century AD, the Greek author Paladius went so far as to illustrate how best to fatten them.

The black-necked pheasant (scientific name *Phasianus colchicus*) is known to have been taken westward to France and to Great Britain by the Roman legions, but it was not sighted in central Europe, in the Rhine Valley, until the thirteenth century, and as far north as Denmark until 1562. The Chinese ring-necked pheasant was a much later introduction. Their iridescent winter plumage soon made the cock pheasant the star of all game birds, and the way in which they adapted themselves to the European countryside quickly gave them an impressive reputation. Without the pheasant population as it is in Europe today, shooting would be considered by many as a dull sport – for included with every type of game bird shot, pheasant now account for at least 90 per cent of the entire bag.

Although the advent of the shotgun had much to do with the development of the sport of pheasant shooting, the date when the bird was first hunted for that reason remains a mystery. Old English sporting literature does, however, have many accounts of the early days of pheasant shooting with flintlock muskets, a somewhat different game to the sport as we know it today. 'It is just as easy to hit a pheasant when it is flushed,' stated one sportsman at the end of the eighteenth century, 'as it is to hit a flying haystack.'

Several methods of shooting pheasants evolved during those early years, not least being Ludwig VIII of Hessen-Darmstadt's idea to lamp them in their roosts at night. Employing men armed with mirrors and bright lanterns he could achieve a considerable bag by shooting them out of the branches, and he must be regarded as the mentor of the modern professional poacher (as illustrated on page 78). The improved and more sporting method of walking up pheasants only came into its own when there were enough sportsmen within reach by foot or pony cart to make a day's shooting worthwhile, and for a long time most pheasants were shot by individual marksmen, particularly in the spring when cock pheasants are so engrossed in fighting over their ladies that they make easy targets on the ground.

J. J. Shaddick

Although the Asiatic pheasant has been a native of Europe for hundreds of years, and in America since its introduction just before the turn of the twentieth century, many naturalists, on both sides of the Atlantic, still regard the pheasant as a foreigner.

It is said that the first birds may have been captured by the Argonauts when they visited Colchis in search of the Golden Fleece, releasing them into the wild upon returning to Greece. The first reliable information on this European pheasant, the black-necked

Finders keepers!

Walking up pheasants in a wet field of kale is an experience few are likely to forget, certainly until they have reached a hot bath. Pheasants love kale but, because other cattle feeds have largely replaced the crop, it may be necessary for a shoot to subsidise the farmer to ensure that it is still grown

20

'SHOOTING FLYING'

The breech-loading shotgun, introduced during the middle of the nineteenth century, presented the sportsman with a different set of options. At last he was able to nail a bird in the air with some degree of accuracy, and for the first time it gave him confidence to shoot at driven game birds, a sport which soon came to be known as 'shooting flying'.

As a result of this change in shooting methods, which many initially considered to be unsporting, the intensive rearing and releasing of pheasants became an accepted part of the country scene, thus encouraging more rural employment and a thriving shooting industry. Today, those nations that have been far-sighted enough to have preserved their field sports intact derive valuable foreign earnings from driven pheasant shooting, particularly countries such as Hungary and Czechoslovakia.

It is said that shooting in Hungary goes back to

The rise by Rankin

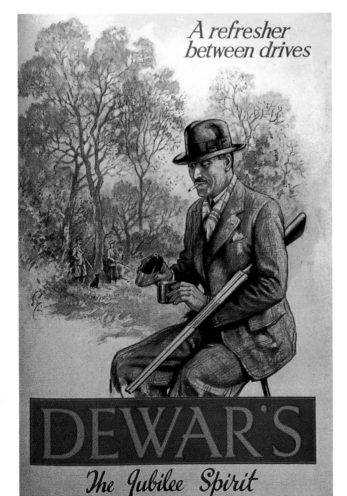

A refresher between drives

DEWAR'S
The Jubilee Spirit

when Hunor and Magor, after following a white stag, found themselves in a paradise so rich in game that they founded the Hungarian nation. Generally, although large bags were the exception rather than the rule in Great Britain, prodigious numbers of birds were already being shot on the Continent. During December 1909 it was recorded that eight Guns shooting on Count Louis Karolyi's estate in north western Hungary killed 6,125 pheasants in one day, and in 1939, shortly before the start of World War II, 289,000 pheasants were shot in Hungary, together with more than a million partridges, in one season. After the war the pheasant population in Hungary declined for a time, but by the 1980s it had increased again considerably, so that now there are an estimated 2.5 million pheasants within the country's borders, of which some 45 per cent are reared annually. The deliberate planting of game cover in

Hungary and Czechoslovakia can be assigned to no particular date, but well sited 'remises', or spinneys to hold game, are known to have existed long before the nineteenth century. Today pheasant shooting on their vast undulating plains follows many of the same procedures. Shooting parties are usually invited to stay in traditional hunting lodges and each day beaters send pheasants flying from large blocks of woodland or flush them from 'remises' which provide the best quality birds. As in Western Europe, such sport, particularly as a form of business entertainment, is becoming increasingly popular.

Popularity breeds contempt and many true sportsmen believe that the prices now asked for driven pheasant shooting are ludicrous. However, because of rapidly escalating costs, those pheasant shoots that fail to find paying Guns may soon be just a memory. In Great Britain during the Edwardian era, as mentioned later, as many as 3,000 pheasants might be bagged in a single day. Most sportsmen hope that such days never return and that pheasant driving will remain an art (see page 86) rather than just a business excuse for a *battue*, or wholesale slaughter.

'Just let 'em try. I'm sitting this one out!'

THE HIGH AND MIGHTY

Pheasants by Rickman

Shooting can never be an exact science, and were it so, few of us would ever wish to shoot again. No game bird proves the point better than the ubiquitous high pheasant.

Although on flat ground it may be possible to encourage pheasants to rise well above the tree line by placing stops at a flushing point inside the trees and flaggers between the trees and the Guns, the result may sometimes seem a little artificial. Genuine high pheasants belong only to steep country, where it is possible to drive them from hill to hill across deep valleys, and where quality not quantity is the measure of success. The county of Devonshire, in south west

England, is one of the best known regions for shooting high pheasants, and those who have shot there, or in other hilly areas, tend to go there every season – either to repair their shattered confidence or to boost their already mighty reputations.

Top pheasant shots are no longer judged, as they were in Edwardian times, on the number of birds they are capable of eliminating in a day; it is more likely that they are assessed on the number of high birds missed – and that depends on a combination of diverse factors that few have ever attempted to grasp. One of these, the famous Edwardian Sir Ralph Payne-Gallwey, wrote a book on the subject, *High Pheasants in Theory and Practice*, which, for a time, became the blueprint for all ambitious pheasant

Over the tops by Armour

The small target provided by a 40yd pheasant is an illusion. Sir Ralph Payne-Gallwey once pointed out that the apparent size of a low, crossing bird is considerably larger

shots. 'It is often argued,' he wrote, 'that if a shooter leans backwards and fires at a high overhead pheasant after it has passed him, he is more likely to score a kill by reason of the shot-pellets entering the bird under its feathers. This is a curious supposition, as the shooter – if his spine did not break – would require to bend backwards at 45° to penetrate the feathers, which overlap on a pheasant like the slates on a roof.' Payne-Gallwey, who was one of the great exponents of taking a bird well out in front, continued later in his book: 'First quickly realise its line of flight, then, with the required amount of forward allowance, swing the gun in the direction the bird is flying and pull the trigger, if possible, without consciously checking the movement of the gun' – which, I suppose, is not the same as following a pheasant through its head, as we all learned at shooting school. Payne-Gallwey based his calculations on pheasants flying to a height of 40yd (36.5m) or 120ft. 'I cannot put any of the exceptionally high birds which I shot myself as being over that height,' he declared.

A high left and right. (The falling birds are reflected in the puddle.)

Aim off on a calm day with a bird flying at a normal speed of 40mph (69kph):

at 30yd (27m)............. 7ft (2m)
at 35yd (32m)............. 8ft (2.5m)
at 40yd (37m)............. 9ft (3m)

'To have a good chance of killing a high pheasant at least seven pellets should strike it, as not more than two are likely to penetrate a vital part,' he deduced from examining dead birds he had hoisted to various altitudes by kite, and he found in consequence that the size of shot had little bearing on velocity and penetration but that it was the spread of the shot that really mattered. Also he discovered that a No 6 shot was likely to be more efficient than the larger No 4 and No 5 shot (which do not pack as many pellets) 'Too often a pheasant may be hit by a few pellets from a large number of shots, without bringing it down.'

Today the high pheasant remains just as testing as ever, and the number of Guns that could down forty birds with successive shots (as once recorded by Payne-Gallwey) must still be minimal. However, there are certain marksmen who, not necessarily agreeing with Payne-Gallwey, pursue pheasants at even greater altitudes with heavy load No 5 'Tigers' fired through multichoke 30in (76cm) barrels, with impressive determination. Many would regard this as taking pheasant shooting too far and, because of the increased risk of wounding birds, such practice is no longer considered 'cricket'.

25

DOGGING GROUSE

Walking up grouse over pointers

Opposite: On the grouse moor

The red grouse is an extraordinary bird for not only is it unique to the British Isles but, unlike any of the rest of its wide ranging cousins, it never changes into winter clothing. Not content with that, although it makes its home in the moorland heather, it is now reluctant to breed on any moor in the southern half of England.

The annual pilgrimage north is for most British marksmen the most stimulating occasion in the whole shooting calendar. Armed with shotguns and cartridges and sometimes accompanied by trusty

pointers, the traditional way to travel has always been on the overnight sleeper. Waking up to a view of the Yorkshire moors or of the rugged hills of Scotland must be a sensation close to that of arriving in paradise.

There are three ways of shooting grouse – walking them up, shooting them over dogs, or driving them. Each method has its separate merits and its own enthusiastic band of supporters, but few of them are more ardent than those who go dogging.

Shooting purists may scorn the 'doggers', for a grouse flushed from the heather seldom makes the shot of the century, but dogging is as much about the approach to the bird as stalking is about the approach to the stag, and both are equally exhilarating. What can be better on a summer's day than to climb the hill and spy a pointer, tail stretched and nose jutted, as it scents grouse hiding amongst the peat-hags ahead. The handler whispers, the dog inches forward, crouching low, its silhouette like a bronze statue

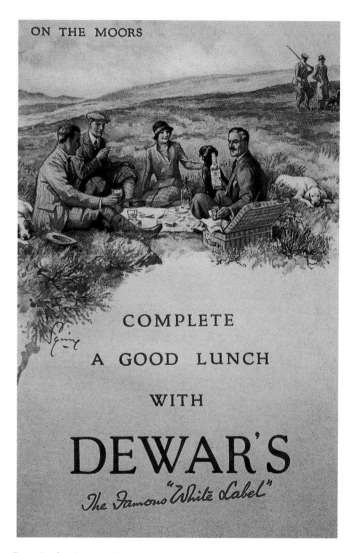

ON THE MOORS

COMPLETE

A GOOD LUNCH

WITH

DEWAR'S

The Famous "White Label"

Dewar's advertisement of 1934

against the mauve backdrop of heather. 'G'back, G'back', shout other birds alarmed by the stealthy approach of the two Guns moving just in front and to either side. But the warning goes unheeded until, with a frantic whirr of wings, the covey explodes into the air like a feather firework.

DRIVEN GROUSE

Although prodigious bags of grouse have been taken while walking them up with dogs, it being recorded that on the 'Glorious Twelfth' day of August 1871, the first day of the season, the Maharajah Duleep Singh accounted for no less than 440 grouse to his own gun, most grouse are shot from the 'butt'.

Wing of old grouse

Wing of young grouse. Young grouse make better eating

During August 1913, an American journalist, reporting on the sport of grouse driving, commented: 'Mr Remington Wilson, of Broomhead, England, is modestly receiving the congratulations of his friends. With eight guns he has "broken the record" by shooting 2,748 Grouse in one day. Counting ten hours' work, which is about what union rules allow, the nine guns must each have averaged one bird killed in a little less than two minutes. The birds were practically tame: they had been looked after by keepers from the day they were hatched. Even fright was kept out of their experience of life – until the day when they were driven by beaters up the blind, where concealed shooters sat in comfort, with refreshments at hand and plenty of men to load their spare guns.'

The truth is that shooters rarely sit in comfort as, unless there is a pleasant breeze blowing, they spend much of the time defending themselves against the hordes of attacking midges. Refreshments are at a premium, unless they are laboriously carried forward to the 'front line', and then there is no time for drinking, let alone for sighting the rapidly approaching packs of grouse – as they 'bomb' the butts with suicidal determination.

Red grouse are, in reality, so wild that it would not be possible, as our journalist suggests, to tame them. Keepering is not a matter of collecting and hatching eggs but more a business of controlling vermin and burning heather in order to encourage the young shoots for the grouse to feed on. They are territorial

A line of butts, well constructed from rock and peat, topped with heather

birds whose numbers may vary dramatically from year to year largely due to a virus, louping ill, carried by sheep tick and a parasitic worm, which causes a disease called strongylosis. Grouse are not blessed with a long duration of flight, but they tend to hug the contours at great speed, avoiding suspicious objects with rapid changes of direction, and providing only an occasional high shot from a low sited butt (see page 87).

Bombing the butts. The fast, low-flying grouse provides a varied and challenging target. Grouse shooting, which is a sport unique to the British Isles, ends on 10 December

BLACK GAME

Black game by Thorburn

Now whistlin' winds and slaught'rin guns
Bring autumn's pleasant weather,
The moorcock springs, on whirring wings,
Among the blooming heather.

ROBERT BURNS

Black game, otherwise called black grouse (or once better known as moorcock), is one of the rarest but most interesting birds to be found in the British Isles. Native to most moorland areas of England for many thousands of years, only during the last century has the bird become extinct in all but a few northern counties and in parts of Scotland. Thirty years ago it was estimated that there were more than 10,000 breeding pairs of black game, some living as far south as Devonshire, but now the number has dropped to less than a third. Northern gamekeepers, aware that the bird is under threat, often have a soft spot for them. 'Red grouse are my living,' stated one keeper, 'but black grouse are my hobby.' Like the red grouse they survive, apart from insects, mainly on a diet of young heather, bilberries and conifer shoots, and as forestry, with its attendant stock of vermin, and farming land, with its overgrazing and its vile dosage of sprays, have encroached on their natural habitat, the stock has either been killed, has died out or has moved elsewhere.

Unlike the red grouse, its black brother and sister – the blackcock and greyhen – are to be found in other northern European and Asian countries, the male of the species being considered by some as the most magnificent-looking game bird of all. They are considerably larger than red grouse and, tending to prefer mature woodlands to open moor, they may often be seen in winter on the fringes of the woodlands feeding on the leaf buds. As one Scandinavian ornithologist put it: 'The sight of a flock of these heavy and beautifully shaped birds, grouped like large fruit in the branches of a birch whitened by hoar frost, is one of the most splendid spectacles I know.' Black game, however, are far more famous for their courting displays. In early spring the males may be seen on a log, a peat hag or other conspicuous spot seeing off their rivals. Then, watched by a crowd of females, the blackcock will strut around the spot selected – known as a 'lek' – trailing its wings, puffing up its throat and neck, and displaying the snow white feathers that fan from under its lyre shaped tail.

It is said that later in the season, which starts on 1 September, black game can provide some of the finest driven shooting for, despite their size, they are extremely agile. But, because the summer moult will have left the males devoid of tails, and the young too confiding, early shooting, combined with red grouse driving, may take a heavy and unnecessary toll. Bags in southern Scotland once consisted of one black grouse for every ten red grouse shot, but today, in Great Britain, this bird of many names is more often than not left alone.

Blackcock by Harrison

Love dance for a lady watching at the lek

CLIMBING FOR PTARMIGAN

Haunter of the herbless peak
   Habitant 'twixt earth and sky
Snow-white bird, of bloodless beak
   Rushing wing and rapid eye
Hath the fowler's fatal aim
   Of thy freeborn rights bereft thee,
And mid natures curbed or tame
   Thus encaged, a captive left thee?
Thou who, earth's low valleys scorning,
   From thy cloud-embattled nest
Wont to catch the earliest morning
   Sunbeam shining on thy breast!
D. M. Moir

Ptarmigan live above the tree line, at no lower than 2,000ft (600m). The smallest of the grouse family, the common ptarmigan is to be found not only in Scotland, but also in the Alps, the Urals and the Pyrenees, and its close relation, the rock ptarmigan, in the mountains of Iceland, Greenland, North Eastern America and Japan. A third variety, the white-tailed ptarmigan lives high in the tops of the Rocky Mountains, stretching from Alaska to New Mexico.

How the birds survive in these hostile regions seems to defy nature. But picking at the lichens, often covered by snow, they somehow manage to eke out

"GERALD BUXTON, ONE OF THE MOST INTREPID AND DETERMINED OF MEN, COULD NOT STAND THE STRAIN OF THIS TERRIBLE JOURNEY, AND DID MOST OF IT ON HIS HANDS AND KNEES"

Ptarmigan are sometimes a difficult quarry

a meagre existence, often perching on rock or scree exposed by the wind.

Living in these remote heights, and seldom seeing man, they have almost no fear of him. Their first instinct is to squat and keep still because of other enemies, but after a short time the birds will often strut about, or fly in circles, like tame pigeons. Their only 'preservative' is probably their clever camouflage, which blends with the rock in summer and the snow in winter. Many imagine that the birds' brilliant white winter plumage grows after the summer moult but, surprisingly, experiments have shown that it is more a case of its feathers fading in colour than the provision of an entirely new jacket. It is also interesting that this jacket, because of its colour, loses heat at a much slower rate than, for example, its Scottish neighbour, the red grouse.

Shooting is not to be numbered among the pressures facing ptarmigan, which more concern other predators and the continuing loss of Alpine vegetation. During the nineteenth century, however, the English regarded climbing for ptarmigan as an almost heroic sporting achievement – which it probably was, considering transport arrangements at that time. The advent of the railways in the Highlands made such expeditions much easier, but there is nothing soft about scaling the dizzy heights after ptarmigan, and nothing more rewarding, to the few who attempt it, than bagging perhaps just one bird in such magnificent surroundings.

Ptarmigan by Thorburn

Climbing for ptarmigan

NORTH AMERICAN GROUSE

American grouse

The North American grouse family is wide ranging, of varied habits and of uncertain lineage. The graceful dusky grouse of the Rocky Mountains has an entirely different life style to the sage grouse or cock-of-the-plains. The ornate pinnated grouse, with his two bright yellow sacks on the sides of his neck, seems an unlikely relation of the dowdy spruce grouse of the colder north. But champion bird of the family is undoubtedly the flamboyant ruffed grouse.

Ruffed grouse are often seen by deer hunters as the birds prefer to live in woodlands, particularly where there are birches and plenty of undergrowth. They enjoy picking at berry-bearing shrubs and in the fall, when they themselves are hunted, usually with dogs, they may be found, singly or in small coveys, scouring the hills for beech nuts or the valleys for the seeds of skunk-cabbage. Intelligent birds, they are by no means easy to shoot, leaving the ground with hardly a sound and slipping away on silent wings, weaving and dodging through the trees. No wonder that their territory still stretches from Canada to the Southern States and that they somehow manage to survive in the heavily hunted coverts of New Jersey, Connecticut and Pennsylvania.

The distant sound of drumming, to some, may be synonymous with the wilderness, and following it may lead both man and mate to the ruffian of the forest, the male ruffed grouse. With his ruff raised like some ancient courtier, yellow skin flushed with pride, he may be found, tail fanned out, drumming on his favourite log to attract the attention of the females. Although, surprisingly, drumming is a year-round activity, it is heard mostly when the snow melts in the spring. The sound is actually made, normally at intervals of about four minutes, when the bird leans back on his tail and strikes his wings against the wind, and for fired up drummers, who may drum at intervals of less than a minute, it is such a strenuous exercise that in the courting season they will lose a great deal of weight.

The drumming log: two male ruffed grouse compete for a bride

Grouse hunting in America, late nineteenth century

DESERT GROUSE

The sixteen species of sandgrouse, which live mostly in the desert regions of the world, are a remarkable class of birds. When on the wing they much resemble pigeons, tending to fly in flocks, particularly when looking for water or migrating, a habit practised by all but a few.

During the mid-nineteenth century sandgrouse were seen on the east coast of England and sandgrouse nests were discovered in Holland and Denmark. There was a great visitation of sandgrouse to Europe in 1888, although they never established themselves; their summer habitat now extends more from the Kirghiz Steppes in Central Asia to Mongolia and Northern China.

One of the most beautiful of the species, Smith's sandgrouse (*Pterocles gutteralis*), which in late winter is found on the east coast of Africa from the highlands of Abyssinia to as far south as the Transvaal, makes good eating but, like the yellow-throated sandgrouse, which is the largest and by far the most sporting member of the family, it is usually no challenge to shoot at all.

First place the hawk on his perch, then take aim and blow out the feather sand stopper – probably the only sporting way of shooting sandgrouse!

Sandgrouse

37

BOBWHITE

'You can't hit a man in the tail like a quail'
From 'Annie Get Your Gun'

Of all American game birds none is better known or more loved than the partridge, as he is called in the south and west of America, or in other parts of the United States, as the bobwhite quail. In fact the bobwhite (*Colinus virginianus*) is neither partridge nor true quail, for his European quail cousin is a dumpy little fellow with dull plumage and rather ordinary habits. It is said, indeed, that this bird,

Quail

which is somewhat sluggish in flight, has, while migrating south to Africa, crossed Italy in such prodigious numbers that up to one hundred thousand birds have been shot within just a few miles of the coast *(Daniel's Rural Sports)*.

Although bearing no resemblance to the common grey partridge, it is true that the bobwhite looks rather like his cousin the red-legged Frenchman but here, Americans would argue, the similarity ends. That their bird flies faster and over longer distances, may be correct, but they do form coveys or 'bevys', the males are monogamous (like partridges, keeping to their wife and brood until each following spring),

and their wing feathers are more akin to those of partridges than quail. But one habit is very different – for they are champion runners, and when they semi-migrate south and east during October (the height of the European partridge shooting season) they are useless to hunt because they flatly refuse to take to the air. Only after they have returned later in November do they present any sport at all.

'It is a singular proof how strong is the passion for the chase and the love of pursuit implanted by nature in the heart of man, that however much we deprecate the killing of these little birds with their plaintive call,' wrote an American, Frank Forester, 'the moment the dog points and the bevy springs – all the

Hunting bobwhite – the game bird of America

compassion is forgotten in the eagerness and emulation which are natural to our race.'

Possibly the best quail shooting is to be found in North and South Carolina, Georgia, Alabama and Texas, but there are many other good areas besides. Quail tend to flush as one bird and then fly, often from stubble, at high speed to the nearest thicket. A good hunting dog is more or less essential and then, once the bevy has been split into single birds, the bobwhite can provide an extremely sporting shot.

Scattering a bevy of quail

BOOMING CHICKEN

No chicken!

Sharp-tails or square-tails, what is a prairie chicken? Many old-timers would insist that the only true 'chicken' is the pinnated grouse, or square-tail, but the term is generally applied to two different species of grouse that live out on the open prairie, and gourmets would argue that the sharp-tail is the better bird, particularly when broiled over a hot bed of charcoal.

During the winter prairie chicken tend to form into packs, sometimes of several hundred birds, and when spring comes flocks of both species will adopt their own 'booming' or duelling grounds, each on some dominant feature about the size of a tennis court. Out on the Great Plains duelling between the males will often begin before dawn and for hours the square-tails will strut and lunge at each other, while the sharp-tailed grouse do an acrobatic sabre dance high above the prairie grass. As the fighting grows to a frenzy, the cocks raise their antenna-like head-dresses and, filling and emptying their orange neck pouches with air, they will emit such an eerie call that it may attract a harem of admiring females from as much as a mile away. Some booming grounds may be shared simultaneously by both sharp-tails and square-tails, but as more males try and join the pageant the master cocks will fiercely repel all boarders.

The booming ground

The traditional way of hunting prairie-chicken was to load up a spring wagon with bedding, food for three days, cooking gear, two or three hundred pounds of ice, guns and ammunition and a crate of 'bird dogs', and then to set off with a team of 'broncs' into the wilds of the Prairie. Throughout the wheat-lands, wherever the ground is too wet to plough, may be found patches of willow and popple known as 'clumps' or 'bluffs', and by moving from one to another, particularly on a warm day, prairie-chicken were never too hard to find. But sadly the horse and buggy have now been replaced by the motorised 'pickup', and many packs of birds have declined considerably. As one old hunter said: 'You rode when you wished and walked until you were glad to ride again. Stop and kill a rattler or crouch in the grass to down a hawk. It was all part of a great game that the hunter of today can never know.' Nor, for that matter, can the poor old booming chicken!

Prairie dust-up

EMINENCE GRISE

The fields of stubble enjoyed by the prairie chicken might also have suited the distinguished grey partridge – except that, unlike his French red-legged cousin, he does not greatly relish the heat. For the grey partridge, popular long before the pheasants' triumphant progress through Europe, is the classic game bird of the open fields. Its general habitat reaches to the edge of cultivation with a natural distribution ranging 62° north and south to the Pyrenees, west to Ireland, where they are now almost extinct, and east as far as the Altai mountains in outer Mongolia.

Partridge and chicks. Ground cover in the British Isles is fast disappearing

Thirty years ago it was estimated by Great Britain's Game Conservancy that there were some 120 million grey partridge in the world, but today the population has diminished to less than 20 million. Earlier counts are not so reliable but there are tales of large numbers of partridges being shot for sport as far back as the seventeenth century:

> See how the well-taught pointer leads the way!
> The scent grows warm: he stops – he springs
>   the prey;
> The flutt'ring coveys from the stubble rise,
> And on swift wing divide the sounding skies;
> The scatt'ring lead pursues the certain sight,
> And death in thunder overtakes their flight.
>   GAY

– no wonder the partridge has had such a thin time; but the actual cause of the birds' decline was neither the flintlock nor the modern shotgun.

The practice of walking up partridges over open ground, often with a pointer, has always been particularly sporting, for the birds have such keen eyesight that it is usually most difficult to get near them. One method was to keep them pinned down by flying a kite with the appearance of a hawk, but if the wind was strong enough for kite flying, the partridges also flew like bullets and were seldom shot. In the good old days sportsmen would walk more than a mile for every bird bagged and similarly driven grey partridge have an uncanny knack of being almost as elusive.

The much publicised pressures affecting the partridge population start and end on the farm. Intensive farming methods have reduced the number of hedgerows and limited stubble fields to such a short period between harvest and plough, that the birds have hardly enough time to fill their crops with the gleanings. By September, when the partridge shooting season begins, little stubble may be left, but any insects – a vital ingredient of the young birds' diet – which have somehow escaped being killed by insecticides, are soon buried under the soil. Even headlands of rough vegetation are no longer left for the birds to nest in during the spring, and there is such a lack of weed seed that the poor partridges have not much left to live on. Good reason for partridges to feel a little grey at times!

Four white partridges, shot on Lord Hastings' Melton Constable Estate in 1908

Partridges have such keen eyesight that it is often difficult to get near them

DRIVEN PARTRIDGE

Taking them early

Partridge driving, first recorded in Great Britain in about 1845 (Gladstone), soon became as much rooted in the land as any other traditional country sport; the record British bag, shot as recently as 1952 on the late Sir Joseph Nickerson's Rothwell Estate, Lincolnshire, being of 1,059½ brace. But so great has been the general decline in partridge numbers latterly, particularly in Eastern Europe, that in many parts of the world the birds are no longer driven.

In 1913, shortly before the beginning of World War 1, more than a million partridges were shot in Hungary alone. Partridge trapping had long been a way of life in the old Austro-Hungarian Empire, and so many birds and eggs had been exported to other parts of Europe and beyond for restocking, that the grey partridge had come to be known universally as the 'Hungarian'. But by 1972 the number of partridges shot in Hungary had dropped to just one hundred thousand, and today with an annual bag of less than ten thousand, partridge driving in Hungary is no longer a commercial proposition. The finger is pointed directly at the Hungarian government – for by breaking up the traditional family farms and creating huge fields of monoculture, they left little sanctuary for the birds to survive in. This, combined with the increased application of toxic sprays, a universal problem, produced a devastating result. Indeed it is now believed that the partridge population has declined dramatically not only in Hungary, but in all thirty-one countries of the world in which it is found.

The hand-rearing of partridges may have helped to maintain stock at certain levels but although they fly nearly as well as wild partridges, they are born with little territorial instinct, making them inclined to stray and awkward to handle during the shooting season. As partridges are not quite so easy to rear as pheasants, being poor layers in captivity, it is unlikely that they will ever be reared in sufficient numbers to halt the downward trend – particularly as they

Partridge driving, circa 1920

become as bad at looking after their broods as every other species of semi-domesticated game bird.

One of the attributes of the wild partridge is its willingness to stay conveniently to hand when shooting is going on. One does not lose wild partridge for the day, as is the case with grouse, which may sometimes remain absent for ever; partridge often return within a few hours to the place from which they were first flushed. They are superb sporting birds, able to fly many times from field to field without apparent exhaustion (see page 88). But although an excuse for driving them was that out of any covey the old cock birds and barren 'pairs' were always shot first, such justification is hardly necessary. Grey partridge have remarkable manoeuvrability, and the instant that they see the line of Guns they present the ultimate close-range sporting target, flaring and changing direction with a breathtaking turn of speed.

First drive of the day. The Guns stand back in a hollow on a misty October morning

PARTRIDGES IN SPAIN

providing outstanding sport. Partridge driving begins in Spain in mid-October, the finest shoots being situated well away from intensive farming areas – ideally over a mix of one-third *monte* (scrub covered hills) and two-thirds thin cereal ground, olive groves and vineyards. As demand for partridge shooting has increased, the sport has spread ever deeper into the Spanish countryside, and the most favoured area now stretches from Toledo, in the centre, to La Mancha, in the south. In some districts, such as Ciudad Real, bags on well managed estates may average one bird per acre (2 to 3 birds per hectare), particularly in the sherry region of Jerez, where some drives may cover more than 1,000 acres (400 hectares) of land, women, horses, fighting bulls and shooting partridges are a man's whole way of life.

The lifestyle of the Spanish partridge is also not so bad, and preferable to that of other members of his species – as unsprayed insects, sometimes augmented by game crops, provide an abundant supply of food, and he is unlikely to be driven over the Guns more than two or three times each season. But moisture, a major attraction to partridges, is often more of a problem. Predators must also be controlled by the keeper, or by hired specialist vermin-killers (*bicheros*), and these may include foxes, magpies, wild cats, weasels, polecats, eyed lizards and certain snakes. Wild boar can also be a particular menace to partridge stocks.

Partridges are shot in Spain by at least ten to twelve Guns each shooting with a pair of guns, carried between stands by an experienced *cargador*, or loader. Also in attendance is a *secretario*, or picker-up, and it may be his additional job to conceal the Gun, possibly with a roll of green canvas or by adding some fallen branches. Guns are positioned to provide the most challenging shooting, and shot-proof safety shields may sometimes be erected between each position. Hidden behind the shields on a hot day the Duke of Alba once nodded off. 'Please don't worry about it, senor Duque,' whispered his diplomatic *secretario*, 'you will find fifty partridges laid out by your butt.'

Partridge drive in Spain

Nearly all the partridges of the hot countries are variations of the red-legged partridge, *Alectoris rufa* – for the related chukar, the African Barbary partridge, the rock partridges of Italy and the Spanish or French partridge, can all interbreed. Hybrid red-legged partridges are, however, now so discouraged in England that restocking with them, which has been going on for many years, could soon be illegal. Those wishing to shoot a 'Frenchman' may then have to travel to Spain.

Fortunately in Spain red-legged partridges suffer few of the agriculturally induced hazards that affect the bird in other parts of the world, and as long as they are not over-shot and their enemies are controlled, stocking up with French hybrids will be unnecessary, and will be practised solely by those who are greedy. The wild Spanish partridge is, indeed, a law unto itself and (unlike the grey partridge) apart from its tendency to run or to perch in trees when flushed it flies rapidly in a straight line,

Red-legged partridges, driven from the shade of rocks and olive trees, dip swiftly over the guns

COCKS OF THE WOOD

The close season for capercaillie in Great Britain is not determined by the Game Act of 1831, as with other game birds, but by local authority orders, the reason being that there were none of these glorious birds remaining in the country at that time. The once indigenous capercaillie, or capercailzie, a word derived from the Gaelic *capull coille*, meaning literally 'horse of the wood', had by the 1760s already been hunted out of existence, and only after repeated attempts by a number of enthusiasts was the bird reintroduced – principally by Lord Breadalbane, who

in 1837–8 imported a large number of capercaillie eggs and young 'cocks of the wood', as they had been renamed, from Sweden. The 'caper', which is the bird's more familiar title today, has never, fortunately, found a guaranteed place in British game books either, although it is written that a shooting party, which included the Duke of Atholl, Count Clary and the Marquis of Tullibardine, shot a record bag of sixty-nine capers on 4 November 1910 at Dunkeld in Perthshire. It is true that for a considerable time after their reintroduction the birds multiplied strongly, particularly in the ancient Caledonian pine forests of Scotland, but as the trees were felled the poor caper found little sanctuary, and the numbers have once again declined alarmingly. It is for that reason that many sportsmen will no longer shoot caper in the British Isles.

'No bird, except the ostrich, grows as heavy as the cock capercailzie. Because it is so fat it sits motionless on the ground practically the whole time, and is easily caught by the hunter. It lives in the Alps and northern Europe. It loses its taste in aviaries and it kills itself in old age by holding its breath.' Gaius Plinius (Pliny), when he wrote these words during the first century AD, was one of those early would-be naturalists who considered the capercailzie as being of enormous size, and later, during the Middle Ages, when it had been

Capercaillie by Millais

driven by hunters far into the hills, the bird became semi-mythical, taking its place with the swan, the heron and the bustard as one of the most 'blue-blooded' of all game.

Today the principal haunts of the caper are in the coniferous forests of Scandinavia and Russia, although it is better known as a game bird in the Alps and in mountain areas of central Germany. Here, although many would regard the shooting of displaying birds remarkably unsporting, bagging cock caper in the spring – usually with a small calibre rifle – when such is their bellicose chivalry that they become completely deaf, is, for culling reasons, still 'allowed'. At the Balz-platze, or mating place, the cock caper will fan his tail to the ladies and let out a series of gutteral sounds, known as the *schnalzer*, similar to a cork being drawn from a bottle. This is followed by the *triller*, a number of loud 'clacks', before the bird enters the third phase of his courtship, the *schliefer*, a knife sharpening noise which signals such paroxysms of excitement that he can be approached and shot at will. However he has the last laugh, for those who bag him will find his flesh is as unpleasant as turpentine!

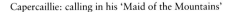

Capercaillie: calling in his 'Maid of the Mountains'

TURKEY SHOOT

Pliny was wrong! The ostrich is not the only bird which is heavier than a cock capercailzie, for wild turkey, sometimes weighing in at as much as 20lb (9kg), may often be double the weight of those splendid 'cocks of the wood'. The wild turkey, which belongs to the same sub-species as the pheasant, is also a forest bird, but, surprisingly, comes from different parenthood than the domestic turkey, its succulent cousin, which was originally imported from Spain. Ranched by Mexican Indians at about the time of the birth of Christ, the wild turkey of eastern North America has never been tamed, is extremely hardy, can run, with a stride of 4ft (1.2m), faster than a bird dog, and can fly at speeds of over 55mph (88kmph).

Wild turkey was abundant when the first settlers arrived in America and it soon went on the menu, being the only important source of meat native to the

Detail of wild turkey heads

New World. Later roast wild turkey became so much a traditional part of Thanksgiving Day feasting, that in 1776 Benjamin Franklin, who obviously appreciated its subtle flavour, proposed that the bird should be adopted as the national emblem of the United States (rather than the American bald eagle). The original domain of the wild turkey covered much of Mexico, most of North America and part of southern Canada, but by 1900, due largely to excessive hunting, it had become almost extinct. In 1948 it was reckoned that the bird had disappeared entirely from fifteen of the states in which it had previously nested, its last stronghold remaining in the swamp lands and mountain regions that were too inaccessible for hunters to approach.

The rescue of the American wild turkey is a lesson in game management that should be recognised by conservationists everywhere. In 1937 two significant steps were taken to save wildlife in the United States, the first being the passing of the Pittman-Robertson Act for wildlife restoration and the second being the formation of The Wildlife Society, which dedicated itself to professional wildlife conservation. By the 1960s determined restocking programmes were already beginning to take effect, and today dramatic increases in the wild turkey population, as monitored

The American wild turkey

by state wildlife agencies, are plain for all to see. But what is more heartening is that, due to growing public awareness and greater state controls on hunting, the wild turkey, except in areas of industrial or agricultural intensification, or in countryside taken over by vermin, may never be threatened again.

Turkey hunting has always been considered a special art but, like stalking caper in the Alps, it is often frowned upon. But those who call wild turkeys to them on the ground with whistles or shoot them when they fly up into the branches to roost, have probably not experienced driven wild turkey. The author once attended such a shoot organised by Adolf Hitler's former head *Förstmeister* in Sennelager, Germany. Most of the imported wild turkeys escaped, but those that were shot struck the ground with such force, that they would have killed anyone they fell on instantly.

Wild turkey prefer shaded woodland or marshy areas

BARNACLE BILL

The third type of heavy bomber in the sporting field is the cunning wild goose. Like other large birds their speed seems often deceptively slow and although they normally fly on a straight course at altitude, which is also difficult to judge, when coming into land they arrive in such a flurry, a tactic known as whiffling, that they may escape the anti-aircraft guns altogether.

The heaviest variety of wild goose is probably the greylag, ganders weighing more than 16lb (7kg) having been recorded in the past (Witherby). Less

Wild goose shooting on a Solway estuary – England, 1920s

1 White-fronted goose; 2 Snow goose; 3 Canada goose; 4 Brent goose; 5 Barnacle goose; 6 Red-breasted goose

weighty, but more flighty, are the barnacles, whose barred feathers make them look particularly handsome. Like many geese the European barnacle breeds as far north as Spitzbergen, but it winters mostly in Great Britain or on the shores of western Europe, particularly along the coast of the North Sea. Here the wildfowler's ability to conceal himself could be sorely tested if, in a few places, old wine barrels had not been sunk into the mud banks between watery roosts and inland feeding grounds – probably at the most sporting point to shoot the geese. The thrill of waiting for the dawn flight is second to none, how ever cold the wind may be blowing off the sea.

Barnacles, more than most, tend to let you know when they are coming and as daylight arrives with its paint palette of pastel colours, the clamour from the skeins of geese rising from the edge of the tide may be reminiscent of the first sounds of the early morning traffic – probably a din one is trying hard to forget.

Barnacle geese whiffling in to feed

GOOSING

Populations of many species of waterfowl, particularly European greylag and pink footed geese, have been greatly on the increase over the past years, for the very same reason that populations of many species of 'land game' have declined. During the seventies and early eighties, as farming became more intensive, increased cereal growing suited the waterfowl population very well, and in some areas, where farmers were inviting sportsmen to shoot the birds as pests, it became necessary to ask for a strict code of conduct. But now that the grain mountains of Europe have influenced the agricultural cereal market to contract once again, the long term future for populations of waterfowl may not be so encouraging.

One area of the world that is unlikely to experience such changing fortunes for the wild goose is northern Mexico. Here, from the beginning of October, hordes of geese arrive for the winter. These are not the Canada goose, seen in such numbers on America's Eastern Seaboard and in the Mid West, but the magnificent white-fronted and snow geese, which not being indigenous to Europe, are found elsewhere only in Russia. The summer rains will have left this region of Mexico awash with endless pools of alkaline water and here, protected by the rolling hills of the *Mesa*, yellowed by meadows of billowing grasses, may be seen such vast flocks of snow geese that they shine in the sunlight like drifting banks of white paper. It is a

Goose-shooting from stubble – Minnesota, USA, circa 1900

sight that no one will forget, particularly those who ride out at dawn on horses, with their saddlebags full of cartridges and tortillas, in order to bring a few home.

Many country dwellers have relied on the flesh of the snow goose at some time in history, and the species' breeding grounds are so far north into the Arctic Circle that during the eighteenth century it was recorded that natives living on the west shore of Hudson Bay would kill as many as five or six thousand snow geese every spring. During the summer in Alaska the wretched birds fared no better, for until they were prevented from doing so at the beginning of the twentieth century, the Eskimos would stretch long lines of nets across the estuaries of the Kuskokwim and Yukon rivers and slaughter snow geese in far greater numbers than would have satisfied any domestic requirement.

Snow geese are shy birds, and because horses cause water-fowl little consternation (a fact unknown to many game wardens), they may often provide the hunter with the safest means of approaching them. Like most wild geese the 'snows' relish water plants and grasses, but are particularly fond of berries, grain – if it is available – and most other kinds of seed. The hunter, having hidden in the marsh grass close to the obvious feeding-grounds, may rely on shooting the geese either as the birds fly over, or with the help of

White-fronted goose

decoys, down them as they are drawn in towards him. Nothing attracts a snow goose as much as another snow goose, but in many places in America, the decoy used is simply a scrumpled sheet of white paper.

Opposite: Snow geese migrate between the Arctic Circle and many states in North America

A flight of Canada geese by Rickman

BOMBAY DUCK

Duck in thousands – Minnesota, USA, 1930s

The shikari

Wildfowl are one of the most fascinating of all the
world's living creatures and they have undoubtedly
captured man's imagination since the beginning of
time. From the orderly routines of their everyday
living to the magic of their dawn and evening flights,
from the beauty of their chosen habitat to the
mysteries of their mass migrations either side of
winter, it is no wonder that members of the family
Anatidae have always held us spellbound, and made
us re-examine our own quality of life every time we
see them flying.

Waterfowl have been part of the mythology of
virtually every civilisation on earth and hunting

became so popular in Egypt at the time of the
Pharaohs that 'marsh tickets' (the first known hunting licences) had to be carried by all sportsmen. Even
today the sky there can be so heavy with duck that
stories of shooting them are likely only to be capped
by those remaining few, who once shot duck during
the days of the Raj in India.

Shooting pintail from a shikari on a lake in India. The pintail is
a freshwater duck in summer but a saltwater duck in winter,
when large flocks of them may be observed, like no other
species, consisting entirely of drakes

Duck flighting, circa 1900

MORNING FLIGHT

A stretch of foreshore, uncovered by the tide,
runs to a jutting headland and a misty horizon
of sea. Levels of sand lie between ledges and
ridges of rock. The sand slopes to the rim of the
tide; there are broad plateaux of rock slippery
with seaweed and bronze bladderwrack, and
opposite, in a gap in the cliff, a rough roadway
for carts and boats. For half a mile out the sea
swings and sways, smooth with floating ice; ice
crusts the foreshore pools, bent and shrunken as
the outgoing tide has drunk each pool lower; the
smell of ice in the wind; from the south a gleam
of sun lights the cliff, the seaweed, the sand.

It is the strip of shore where I shot my first
wild duck, and not even my first grouse survived
in a more vivid setting. Still I see the flicker of
white on his fast beating wings; still his neck
points straight and long; still the sunlight shines
on the green laver of the pool where he fell, the
water sparkles on his throat, his orange feet
splash the ice.

Shooting Days
ERIC PARKER

Oft as the sun's last lingering ray
Gleams faintly o'er the fading scene,
To some still lake we make our way,
And flight the mallard like a dream.
Anon

58

FLIGHTING

An 'original' hide, circa 1800

EVENING FLIGHT

July 9th, 1829 – Made a droll trial of a new stocked duck gun, which was well done by my carpenter Keil. I knocked down, in 7 shots, 6 bats and 1 moth. A duck at dusk flight may therefore know what to expect.

Diary of
COLONEL PETER HAWKER

The magic of the foreshore in the crisp light of dawn can never be matched inland, but as the sport of duck flighting becomes ever more popular, so does the construction of evening flight ponds. Carefully sited where duck may be tempted by extra rations, most ponds are designed with shallow ledges so that the birds may feed in the way that they are accustomed. Farmers, flush with sub-standard potatoes or heaps of barley sweepings, may often invite their friends to an evening's flighting for, unlike more expensive forms of shooting, wildfowling, with little effort, may be enjoyed by everyone.

Duck, like geese, are international birds, spanning estuaries, countries or continents as if scattered by the wind, and true to wildfowling traditions, they are shared by sportsmen everywhere. Commercial flight ponds, where Guns pay to shoot wild birds, are therefore frowned upon, and only the unwritten rules of not shooting duck too hard or too often may save

the birds from wanton destruction. In America the taxpayer now contributes to the conservation of most wildlife, but in Europe such restraint has remained up to the individual. European voluntary organisations have also done a great deal to preserve wildfowl populations, none more than the Wildfowler's Association of Great Britain which was formed well before World War I.

The unpredictability of evening flighting gives the sport an edge of its own – indeed, if feeding is not carried out regularly, no duck may arrive at the pond at all. Much will also depend on the state of the moon, the weather and the time of year. A frosty evening in late autumn with a waning moon may get the adrenalin going, but, if there has been heavy October rain, the ground in the area will be so flooded that the duck may find 'night accommodation' elsewhere. On clear, still, evenings, the birds may often be diffident and difficult to see, but when the wind is blowing the clouds fast across the moon – watch out, for then it is time to go 'ducking'.

It is usual to get to the pond well before sunset, then, as the light fades, and the pheasants clatter into their roosts, it is possible to settle into a hide or creep forward closer to the edge of the water and listen out for the first brave flight of mallard, approaching fast from the dim horizon on whispering wings.

A duck flight by Simpson

THE PUNTER

The fowler by Austen

The punt gunner (origin unknown)

February 1st, 1830 – Off at daybreak A pinching white frost. Saw nothing but some curlews at which my gun missed fire Went ashore to ascertain the cause, and found that some infernal scoundrel had drawn my shot in the night and filled both my barrels with water!

Diary of
COLONEL PETER HAWKER

The origins of laying a bet, or 'punting' on a racehorse, may be obscure, but no explanation seems more likely than that which refers to the dubious sport of punt gunning. Few weapons have been handled with less scruple and greater amateurism, and the chances of a punt gun blowing itself or its owner to bits, can seldom, during their heyday, have bettered 'even money'.

Since the colonel's time improvements in punt design gave 'gunners' no reason for any extra confidence: 'On the Wash', wrote J. Wentworth Day in March 1930, 'round about the Lynn, they use long, narrow, open punts which are little better than floating planks. They are unseaworthy but tremendously fast, and the beginner cannot choose a better way of getting drowned.' Some punts were fitted with leeboards so that a mast and sail could be erected, larger 'rafts' of waterfowl often being found more than a mile from the shore, but the addition of an 8ft long, 60lb (2.5m, 27kg) muzzle-loading shotgun, did nothing for a punt's stability, or for the cramp of the gunner lying frigidly inside.

Punt guns today are regarded more as obsolescent cannon than sensible fowling pieces, and apart from an odd 'bar-oom!', their thunder has most likely gone for good. The old 2-bores, 4-bores and 8-bores fired far more lead than ever seemed necessary, and they were so ponderous to move about, that a punt Gunner needed to have not only Herculean physique but also a great deal of optimism.

Punt gunning, a very technical affair, now largely belongs to a forgotten period

TINY TEAL

And near the mallard you see the lesser dibbling
  teal
In 'bunches' with the first that fly from mere to
  mere
As they, above the rest, were lords of earth and
  air.

DRAYTON

To many the teal is the 'duck of ducks' and if the
dictum 'fine feathers make fine birds' is in any doubt,
it is entirely corroborated by the tiny teal. 'This bird,
for the delicate taste of its flesh', declares Willoughby,
'and the wholesome nourishment it affords the body,
does deservedly challenge the first place among those
of its kind.' What he does not say is that one little
teal hardly makes a meal. The common teal, is in fact
the smallest duck of all. With a wing-span of just 23in
(58cm) and a body length of 14in (35cm), it seldom
exceeds just 11oz (300g) in weight. European or
common teal together with their American cousins –
the green-winged teal, the blue-winged teal and the
cinnamon teal, are also, unquestionably, the most
handsome duck family around.

When teal are disturbed or 'sprung' they do not fly
off into the distance like most other wild duck,
instead they may wheel and weave overhead like an

Duck shooting circa 1840

autumn flight of starlings, returning frequently to
swoop low over the surface of the water before rising
steeply up again, and then, as if by some hidden
signal, dropping back in a staccato series of splashes
– to carry on dibbling. Suspicion is not enough for
teal and they will seldom accept being driven away
for long from their favoured feeding grounds. When
it is close to darkness, and even should the presence
of man be obvious, teal will often commit themselves
to such a hail of gunfire, that to be fair to them,
shooting has to stop. Although teal are erratic
migrators, they also have a reputation as prolific
breeders, and such is their determination to survive,
that once conditions are satisfactory, and without the
lengthy courtship associated with many other species,
they can lay eggs, and set about hatching them,
within just a few days of arrival at the nesting
grounds.

In summer the American green-winged teal, beautiful birds much resembling the European variety, will
nest as far north as Alaska, each rearing as many as
eighteen or more ducklings without much difficulty.
They fly back south in early September, following the
blue-winged teal, and it is then possible to find them
mixed with the mallard and the black duck over most
of the USA, particularly around the marshes and the

shallow lakes of the Western states. However, as the
weather gets colder, the birds will move on again,
following the valley of the Mississippi to the Gulf of
Mexico and further south to the shores of Central
America and the islands of the Caribbean, where, like
other two-legged tourists, they may gather in great
numbers on the sun-bathed beaches.

Shore shooter by Austen

AE.

Hunting green-winged teal on the Laguna Madre, Mexico – one
of the last great coastal wildfowling areas left in the world

DUCK HUNTING

During the 1850s it was estimated that there were some four hundred million duck passing through the United States, but by 1900 numbers had been reduced to half and, during the 1930s, droughts further affected stocks severely. State legislation now varies considerably, but the intention has been to increase close seasons and to limit the number of wildfowl that may be shot. There are several methods of hunting wildfowl in America, but each may depend on the terrain and traditions in various parts of the country. Coastal 'battery shooting', from a well concealed sunken box, was once very popular, as was 'pass shooting', or waiting in 'blinds' (hides) for the duck to fly overhead, but by far the most practised form of wildfowling in the United States remains that of shooting duck or geese over decoys known as 'stools'.

In most states there have always been favoured duck hunting areas, and depending on the amount of sport to be had, a few wildfowling clubs still flourish

A cold morning

Canvas-back, by Rickman

there. One such club, near Boston, had a blind built as an addition to the clubhouse, and when any luckless bird was sighted, a bell, pressed by a lookout, summoned the guns to action, whatever the time of day or night. Clubs, generally, were fitted out with every kind of comfort for the hunter, and professionals were employed, as at golf clubs, to manage blinds, set out stools and to call in the ducks whenever required to do so. Thankfully, however, times have changed, and apart from reduced open seasons and the banning of live stools, duck hunting is now left more up to the conscience of the discerning individual. The customary method is therefore, either to use a well camouflaged 'duck boat', which is taken to the best position and then pulled up on the shore, or to find, or construct, a suitable blind along the saltwater bays or inland waters, and anchor about a

dozen or so wooden stools well within gunshot. Interestingly, these stools have since been developed as a lucrative form of waterfront art – now sold in greater numbers than their 'live models', all over the world.

'Dark lines marked the points of the lake, as yet indistinct; a flock of Duck leaving the surface made the first sound; then the soft whistling of overhead wings. Quietly the boat moved on; finally the blind was reached. Then the few minutes at sunrise, of anticipation, the first silhouettes rising in the east; the first shot, and the splash of a fallen bird. Wet, cold days are recalled, when lying low in the blind was misery, and even the approaching flight failed to warm the soul. Or perhaps, hidden in the ice behind a few stools, waiting at a hole in the open water, too cold to shoot, though Canvass backs [sic] were plenty.'
Reminiscences of a duck hunter from Minnesota

DUCK DOWN UNDER

Along the marsh – Australia, circa 1910

us that 7,000 duck were taken at Lake Rotomahana in the North Island, during just three days. It is apparent that the Maoris were some of the earliest conservationists, and by extending the close season, or *rahui*, for most of the year, they ensured for themselves massive supplies of food. The trick was to drive the duck into the reed-beds during the two months of the summer moult and, because the birds were fat and featherless, it was difficult for them to fly away. Then, in order to preserve the meat, it was packed into bark containers or gourds.

The Australian Aborigines, however, were more sophisticated than the Maoris and collected their duck meat differently. Although they had no close season, they used every device imaginable, including a wide variety of well known weaponry, tame dingo retrievers, nets, and doped pools of water (with a drug called *moru*), to bag their birds, even at times of year when they were flying strongly. They also invented a particularly successful mud camouflage, and in some places were known to take duck from underneath the surface of the water using the stems of reeds as snorkels.

Much of today's duck shooting 'down under' is accomplished with the help of decoys, an idea, surprisingly, never considered by the natives. Black duck are far easier to hoodwink than mallard (with which they sometimes mate), but decoys painted to look like either their own species or the female mallard, which they almost resemble, will normally work for both. Most lakes and billabongs (streams) in eastern

Australia support a resident population of duck for, as in other regions, wildfowl in the Antipodes have little opportunity (or reason) to be truly migratory. A drift of duck does occur, however, during the hot summer droughts, when some birds will fly hundreds of miles to the cooler areas in the south, and it is then that sportsmen may try and bag them, perhaps along the banks of the Murray River, as they pass swiftly overhead.

It is only during the last one-and-a-half centuries that mallard have been introduced to parts of the world outside Europe. Mallard were first brought to the Antipodes in 1867, by the Otago Acclimatization Society, and today it is the most widespread duck in both New Zealand and Australia. Hard on its heels, however, the native black duck and grey teal are equally remarkable – for both species are known to cross the Tasman Sea, between the two countries, quite frequently; a journey of no less than 1,300 miles.

In the same year that the first mallard was released in New Zealand, Sir William Buller, an explorer, tells

Shooting black duck as they drop into cumbungi swamps, in the Australian interior. Black duck fly in straight lines, but in irregular formations, and are unusually strong on the wing. In New Zealand, where a flight of duck is known by the Maoris as a pokai parera, black duck are considered their top game bird

'COCK' SHOOTING

Directly I arrived at the shoot, my host dunned me for half a crown for a sweepstake as to who should shoot the first cock, and I took jolly good care directly I heard the beaters call 'mark Woodcock' – to lie down.

Shooting Stories
GLADSTONE

In 1602 George Owen wrote about the migratory woodcock: 'They are marvellous plentie in cock shoote tyme, wch is twylight, yt is no strange a thing to take a hundred and six score in one wood.' These birds were taken by nets over a twenty-four-hour period, but the largest bag of 'cocks' shot in either England or Ireland, which at one time claimed the record, is only two or three hundred, and therefore bears no comparison.

The British ban on woodcock shooting, during the very cold spells which bring them 'in', has been cause for much disagreement, particularly from the thwarted Guns, for there is no evidence to support the theory that shooting woodcock in frosty weather, or for that matter at any other time, is likely to decimate their numbers badly. On the contrary,

Shooting woodcock circa 1840

woodcock populations in Europe have slightly increased, and to bracket the little bird with waterfowl, which find it difficult to forage through snow and ice, is obviously a misinterpretation of the word 'conservation'. A less agreeable method of shooting woodcock, as once practised in Scandinavia, was that of stalking the male bird in the spring while he was *'roding'* (*la croule* in French), a time when the normally silent fellow sings a croaking love song. Fortunately for the lover this form of hunting has not continued, and as, during the mid-eighteenth century, organised woodcock shoots became more popular on the Continent, some, such as those run by Count de Maroilles, in France, and by Ludwig VIII of Hessen-Darmstadt, in Germany, established far more sporting reputations.

'Woodcocks lays four eggs; they pair, probably have two broods each season, and they are in the habit of carrying the young birds out to the feeding grounds with them. They hold them by various methods: sometimes they clasp them to the breast with the pressure of the bill, sometimes they clasp them between the legs or thighs. One woodcock has been seen to carry two young together, one by each of the methods described.' Such observations were for years considered mere 'flights of fantasy', but the habit has since been noted by so many reliable witnesses that at least the carriage of one chick seems to be true. It is generally believed that wet, mild springs in Northern Europe favour woodcock, which

may also breed in boggy birchwoods or wet scrubland in the British Isles, but the majority of woodcock, which are by nature nocturnal birds, fly to Great Britain and Ireland during the early winter across the North Sea – sometimes guided by the beams from the lighthouses – a tiring flight of several hundred miles.

Woodcock carrying young – by Thorburn

'When the dim twilight slumbers on the glade.' Woodcock love to dart about in semi-darkness, making them difficult targets – often at about head height

THE AMERICAN GENTLEMAN

mortality factors that can be controlled by man and his gun. Today these seasons will much depend on the migratory habits of the bird in individual states, woodcock hunting opening in Canada's New Brunswick from 15 September, but not in America's New England until 1 October. The bag limits are now carefully monitored in North America, and when in 1963 this was raised from four to five birds per Gun per day, interestingly enough it was calculated that, over an average shooting season of fifty days, there was no detrimental effect on the woodcock population whatsoever.

Curiously the American woodcock, which is much smaller than the European variety, is no immediate relation; not if recent findings of fossil bones in

American woodcock enjoy wild, wet woodlands, depicted here in Connecticut, where they are sometimes hunted with pointers. Although over half a million woodcock are shot in the United States every year, numbers, like those in Europe, are increasing slowly

drawn between the Great Lakes and Nova Scotia, in Canada, or from the northern Appalachian Mountains in the United States.

American woodcock, which have a length of only 11in (28cm), are more colourful than their European counterparts, and both males and females sport beautiful cinnamon-coloured breasts. It is said that they are often difficult birds to hunt but, on other occasions, they can be absurdly easy. The woodcock has been called everything from a 'timberdoodle', a 'bog snipe', an 'owl snipe', a 'night partridge' to a 'beetle-eye', but the *Philohela minor* is seldom sworn at – for he is regarded by many sportsmen as the perfect American gentleman.

In 1857 it was stated that, by the use of an artificial light or 'blaze' at night, it was no uncommon experience for one Gun, in Louisiana or Missisipi, to kill 100 woodcock in a single night; this sport being termed 'Fire hunting of Cocks'.

The American Sportsman
Dr Elisha J. Lewis

Before the turn of the twentieth century it was legal, in the United States, to shoot as many woodcock as you wanted, at any time of the year. Subsequently, because of depleting stocks, the Federal Government set strict hunting seasons and bag limits – the only

Florida are anything to go by. It is estimated from these and other evidence that the woodcock was living in America before the last two ice ages, possibly as much as a million years ago; since when his distribution in the United States has not substantially altered. As with the European species, American woodcock seem to prefer shady woodlands and undrained land, having a great partiality for earthworms, which they prise from the damp earth with their extra long bills – as an important part of their diet. These beautiful little birds are therefore to be found principally in the eastern, south eastern, and more forested regions of America, migrating comparatively short distances each winter from a line

'THUNDER BIRD'

It seems ludicrous that such a diminutive bird as the snipe should have been called a 'thunder bird', but so poor was the little fellow's reputation as a harbinger of bad weather, that he was also known as a 'rain bird' or a 'storm bird', although, no doubt, he would refute responsibility for a single cloud.

Chaucer wrote:

All one to thee a falcon and a kyghte,
As good an owl as a popingaye
A dunghill duck as dainty as a snyghte.

A snyghte in Anglo-Saxon meant a snout or beak and only in recent times has the 'snite' – 'a bird lesse than a woodcock' – become known as a 'snipe'.

Snipe are found in all four corners of the world and there are few countries without them. In Great Britain and Ireland there have always been three species of snipe – but only one, the common snipe, will ever nest on home ground. The great or double snipe, however, is rarely seen, and the tiny Jack-snipe, which is entirely migratory, is such an easy shot that it has now, mercifully, been protected. At the turn of the twentieth century it was held that the American Wilson snipe, a close relation, provided such excellent

Snipe shooting circa 1900

hunting in the southern states, that it was matched only by snipe shooting in Burma and in India.

'Many who are good shots at other game', wrote Captain Lacy in 1861, 'find discouraging difficulty in snipe-shooting, else why do they give it up?' Good question, but it could be that some do not like trudging across miles of Irish bog in driving rain all day, to 'chance a snipe'. There are, however, four principal methods of snipe shooting; walking them up, dogging them with a pointer or setter, flighting them at dusk or at dawn, and driving them over standing guns. Snipe driving is no doubt the quintessence of the sport, but bags rarely total more than a miserable percentage of the birds seen, and the brief experience of the bird's weaving, darting flight may be enough for some, it is true, to think of laying up their guns – for ever!

Snipe, because of a mysterious throbbing sound caused by the male's courting habit of swooping down with tail outspread and wings fluttering, were often associated with the supernatural, and in parts of France the female snipe came to be known as the 'Devil's wife'. The American naturalist, Thoreau, said of Wilson's snipe: 'As soon as dusk begins, so that the bird's flight is concealed, you hear this peculiar spirit-suggesting sound, now loud above the din of the village'. Sutton, another American, wrote: 'This weirdly beautiful sound is difficult to describe. "Bleating", it is often called, also "whistling", "winnowing" and even "whinnying", all of which are suggestive, but incompletely so . . .' Today this astonishing and impressive performance is known simply as 'drumming'.

A snipe 'drumming'

Walking up with a gun in Cornwall, an English county renowned for its warm wet weather – the perfect spot for a 'wisp' (or number) of snipe

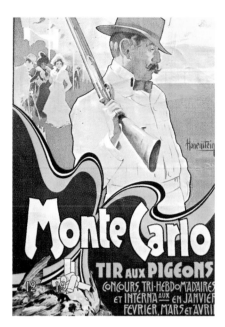

PIGEON PIE

There are principally four accepted methods of bagging pigeons: shooting them over decoys from suitable concealment or hides, intercepting them when they pass overhead on recognised flight paths, waiting for them when they go to roost, or in the case of the wild blue rock pigeon, mainly in the Mediterranean, pursuing them along the cliffs, sometimes from boats. When, however, Captain Lacy wrote during the nineteenth century: 'Pigeon shooting is, unquestionably, the finest practice for the aspirant to excellence in the use of the gun at flying objects,' he was of course referring to the now banned sport of releasing pigeons (rather than clays) from 'traps' – a word still in use today.

Pigeons have always been regarded as pests and there are so many millions of them that it is hard to imagine a country menu devoid of pigeon pie. But numbers do fluctuate and in England during the winter of 1907 so many died of a mysterious disease, that stocks failed to recover for years. Today the pigeon population in England has levelled off, but because additional cash crops are being grown, such as rape and peas, birds are spread over a wider area, and bags of 300 or 400 pigeons a day, as taken in the sixties by British sportsmen, such as the late Archie Coats, are no longer so easy to obtain.

Pigeons, which in summer relish many valuable crops, later particularly enjoy beech nuts. Decoys placed on the sheltered edge of a beech wood are likely to reward any patient sportsmen

Shooting rock pigeons in Malta. Unfortunately the Mediterranean guns are often directed at migrating birds – to the consternation of conservationists

THE PREDATORS

No book on shooting would be complete without a word about the vermin that are the constant plague of the gamekeeper and the occasional pride of the sporting Gun. Hooray for the high magpie or the jinking jay, they often add to the variety of an otherwise predictable day.

It is too easy to be indiscriminate about four-footed vermin, for although the majority of the 'skulkers' and 'prowlers' have no redeeming qualities, there are one or two of them that used to be hunted ruthlessly, but which did very little damage. The badger, which is now protected, was one of the least harmful animals classed as vermin, for often accused of stealing eggs and killing birds, in normal conditions he has always been primarily insectivorous and vegetarian. A different story are the wild mink, which, since escaping from the many mink farms

Weasels

Hen harriers, which may get their name from their polygamous nesting habits, arouse greater anger on the grouse moors than any other hawk in Scotland

Golden eagle

started in Great Britain during the early fifties, have threatened both wild and domestic birds alike – spreading like a plague. Mink now rank high on any gamekeeper's hit list, but of all vermin, none has more crimes to answer for than 'Charlie' the fox. Foxes, depending on the nature of their territory, have tastes ranging from succulent free range chicken to the foul contents of urban garbage bins, but in the depths of the British countryside nothing is more appealing to them than a nesting partridge or pheasant. Foxes, like stoats and weasels, do not kill solely for food, but will often prolong a bloodthirsty slaughtering spree entirely for pleasure. As a result, most British gamekeepers (although mindful of the horse-borne hunting fraternity, who will not have much sport if there are too many foxes) give 'Charlie' a hard time, and in some parts of the country an average of fifty foxes may be shot over 1,000 acres (400 hectares) during just one year. The situation is no different in America, where a survey carried out

in Missouri, for example, showed that over a year one adult fox could easily account for no less than 1,500 quail.

Hawks, which enjoy ever increasing support from the public, have seldom had anything but a bad mark from gamekeepers. Before World War II the disappearance of the hen harrier from most of the British Isles had the same apparent finality as that of the osprey and sea eagle, but although this could have been largely attributed to poisonous seed dressing (soon banned), their sustained recovery during the war years was probably due also to the lack of keepering. Since 1954, when, like other hawks, it was included under the Protection of Birds Act, no predator has aroused greater anger on the grouse moors than the hen harrier, even more than the magnificent golden eagle. Yet, although like its colleague it has a taste for grouse and a propensity for scattering them widely, conservationists say that the hen harrier is not as damaging as some may believe, there being probably no more than 500 breeding pairs throughout Scotland.

Predator control must therefore be maintained on a fine balance – but for those it most concerns, such as agriculturists, gamekeepers, the fur industry and a growing number of conservationists, it is like trying to mix oil and water.

Fox

THE POACHERS

As me and my companions were setting up a
   snare,
'Twas then we spied the gamekeeper – for him
   we did not care,
For we can wrestle and fight, my boys, and jump
   o'er anywhere.

From the ballad of
The Lincolnshire Poacher

The poacher

Left: 'O! 'tis my delight on a shiny night/In the season of the year!'

The hare by Thorburn

Poaching may not be the second oldest profession,
but it must be close to it; certainly it enjoys a similar
kind of disreputable reputation. The poachers themselves, however, do not like to be tarred so easily with
the same brush. There are principally three types of
poachers – the adventurous amateur, the amateur
villain, and the professional villain – and all use
standard poacher's equipment, including the net, the
cruel snare or gin trap for deer, the crossbow, the
silenced .410 shotgun and the silenced .22 rifle.

The adventurous amateur may have started poaching as a child, innocently stealing pheasant eggs or
watching out on shooting days for any unnoticed
casualties. He is seldom without a full-cut coat, to
allow for capacious pockets, and he learns to listen
for a footfall or other warning sounds, and to crouch
in the long grass or crawl along the ditches, fearful
of detection, but full of a sense of excitement. He may
have only bought his coat last night from 'a bloke in
the road' or found a bird that 'hit the telephone
wires', which he put into his pocket till he should
come 'up against the keeper'; but whatever the
excuse, if he has friends in the locality, he will
probably get away with it.

The amateur villain is likely to be a committed
poacher who will stop at nothing – having nothing to
lose. 'He is more often than not a skulking vagabond
who snares or nets for filthy lucre', wrote a former
shoot owner, 'who turns night into day, and is a
drunken domestic tyrant, spending his ill-gotten gains

in some bawdy ale-house.' To this fellow monetary
reward is certainly an incentive, and anyone who tries
to stop him, including the gamekeeper, is likely to
have a pretty rough ride. But somehow there is
always insufficient evidence to bring a conviction
against the poacher, and the game-dealer is always of
'the highest respectability' and did not know from
whom he was buying.

The professional villain, who may be prepared to
shoot at the keeper, is interested only in hard cash.
Working on occasions with other like-minded
citizens, he plans his poaching with ruthless determination and cunning, taking note of the moon, the
wind, local events, local people, and the local
'bobby'. When the wholesale price of game birds is
too low in the shops, the 'specialist' may even turn
his hand to raiding the release pens (mentioned in the
next chapter), for a bird ready for the gun is always
more valuable than a bird ready for the oven! Very
often such bravado does not go unnoticed or un-
punished, but such is the leniency of most British
courts of law, that the professional will probably be
back again tomorrow – a somewhat unsatisfactory
state of affairs.

Large-scale poaching in the nineteenth century, using nets

THE GAMEKEEPERS

The lowland gamekeeper

The old archetypal British gamekeeper, probably once a poacher and certainly Lady Chatterley's lover, virtually no longer exists. W. H. Hudson, a well known nineteenth century naturalist wrote that gamekeepers in his day were so in love with their pheasants that they had the impudence to shoot nightingales for keeping their birds awake at night!

The modern lowland gamekeeper does not have time to listen to the nightingales let alone check that his pheasants are in bed, he is now shooting's managing director and he mans the telephone and the fax machine instead. Some argue that modern gamekeepers are poulterers, and that nature is now left to look after itself, but too much interference in the countryside has never been a good idea, and a nucleus of vermin left alive is better than the whole lot dead. Shoots which before World War II employed six keepers, today may only employ one, and should that keeper be fortunate enough to take on an underkeeper, no doubt it will be because of an increasing number of birds released, and because he has an extended shooting programme to run.

Lowland gamekeepers may now have three different employers, the shoot owner, the paying members of the syndicate and the visiting teams of, often foreign, Guns. His first and last duty must be therefore to please everyone – not forgetting the local pack of hounds.

> If the Guvnors out for birds alone
>   Then birds you mustn't lack.
> You've got ter keep yer foxes down
>   Or else yer gets the sack.
> But if you takes the all round man
>   (Thank ye Sir, mine's a bitter),
> 'E'll 'ave some first-class shootin'
>   As well as many a litter.
>   *A keeper's opinion*
>   H.S.P.

Many of those who enjoy shooting have little idea of the level of planning involved, and the amount of work carried out by the keeper, sometimes with help from volunteers, before the start of each season. The keeper must be both a leader and a diplomat, offering sporting incentives to all who participate, whether in repairing release pens or driving foxes – thus ensuring himself a good team of beaters and pickers-up, when the shoot finally gets into gear.

Unlike the wildlife police forces in America, the French Forest Guards, or the much respected German *Jägermeisters*, all of whom are employed by the state, the British keeper is a law unto himself – but without their powers of arrest. Whereas his French counterpart may seize any weapons and hold a *bracconier*

Pheasant chicks

Eggs in the incubator

The picker-up

human predators and wayward ramblers no easier to control than the extremes of wind and weather.

Members of the Moorland Keepers Association would agree that theirs is a hazardous profession and not one for the faint hearted. Ever conscious of the recurring grouse crises, they must strive to find new ways of protecting the birds and of combating that dreaded parasite the *strongyle* threadworm. Heather burning, the first principle of good 'grousekeeping', can also be laborious, and it must be carried out methodically on a rotation basis by the keeper, preferably in small patches, during the spring of each year. The grouse thrive on tender young heather shoots and growth from earlier burnings also provides them with nesting and escape cover. In Scotland it may take longer than in counties south of the border for the heather to recover. Cover is also essential for the line of Guns, as butts, familiar to the grouse when uninhabited, may, if left in bad condition by the keeper, allow the birds to spy the Guns and turn back over the beaters. It is said that stoats and hooded crows, or even black-backed gulls in places, are the moorland keeper's worst enemy, but because grouse nest unprotected on the ground, 'Charlie' fox can also perpetrate some dreadful massacres. Protected golden eagles and other hawks (see page 84) may not be present in sufficient numbers to do much damage – but that may not be the opinion of the keeper.

A good gamekeeper is also a great naturalist, and by maintaining a careful balance of all living creatures on his patch, his contribution (and that of the sport of game shooting) to the beauty and well-being of the countryside is invaluable.

The larder

The Highland gamekeeper

(poacher) without too much fuss, the British keeper, who is employed on private land, must, as dictated by the 1981 Wildlife & Countryside Act, prove criminal damage, or theft from an enclosed area, before using minimum force (a tap with a heavy stick?) to make an arrest.

None feels more exposed than the moorland gamekeeper, who, often working alone in some of the most isolated regions in Great Britain, finds

SPORTING DOGS

Are pigs better retrievers? Squire Jones' retrieving pig, circa 1810

There are now plenty of dogs bred for game shooting but just as men are mortals, all shooting dogs are mongrels, some more than others true to type. Until shooting became popular as a sport, many breeds, as we know them today, had never been considered, but purpose-breeding quickly followed the development and application of the sporting gun. It is probable that early sporting dogs mostly resembled spaniels, but during the seventeenth century, particularly in Germany, spaniels began to be trained and bred as pointers – dogs which would hold game steady until they were within range of a muzzle-loading gun. The old muzzle-loader was so slow to discharge that, on most occasions, there was little game for a dog to pick up, but later, with the advent of the breech-loader, the retriever, another contrived breed, also came into its own.

The spaniels sporting prowess had long been acknowledged when 'fowling', a general term once used for the pursuit of game birds. Its good reputation continued with the 'net' or 'quarrel', as the crossbow was then called. At first the term 'spaniel' was used for every variety of feathered dog, but as shooting became more popular, two distinct varieties,

the springer and the cocker spaniel, started to emerge. The graceful springer, although never intended for extensive grouse or partridge shooting, was bred primarily to find pheasants in thick coverts, and the smaller cocker, to flush 'cock', or woodcock, as we now call them, from similarly wooded countryside. 'Spaniels for pheasant and cock shooting', stated the Rev Daniels in 1804, 'cannot be too strong, too short upon the leg, or have too much courage. To be in a perfect state of discipline they must always be in their places, twisting around every stub with utmost agility, and possessing such fineness of nose that neither woodcock or pheasant can escape their search.'

Springers were also favoured early on in the United States, but never to the same extent as long-coated setters, also adapted from the spaniel type, which were imported from England or Ireland in considerable numbers during the mid-nineteenth century. Setters soon replaced the old 'settler's dogs', which used to help find upland game for the wagon trains, and together with the pointer, they became the most popular breeds for hunting quail. 'The typical bird dog', wrote an American hunter, 'setter or pointer, should possess above all else, regardless of speed and range, a good nose and bird sense. In general, the pointer learns more readily than the setter to find a bevy of quail, but suffers more from the cold, whereas the setter may be a better dog than the pointer in thick country, although he has a tendency towards acute racial nervousness.'

The retriever

Above: Pheasant well retrieved   *Below*: Snipe retrieved

The other racial dog which immediately gained popularity at home and in the United States was the, then almost always black, Labrador retriever. First imported from Labrador in Canada at the end of the eighteenth century, the Labrador, as the dog came to be known, was primarily a cross between the small black or black and white Newfoundland and the larger setter. 'Capital retrievers have been the produce of very singular crosses', wrote Captain Lacy in

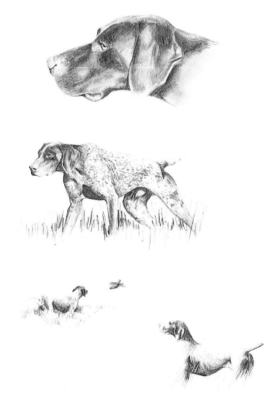

See my pointer stand:
How beautiful he looks! – With outstretched
   tail,
And head immovable, and eyes fast fixed;
One foreleg raised and bent – the other firm,
Advances forward, presses on the ground.
ANON

Action stations!

about 1830. 'One of the best dogs I ever possessed was three parts Newfoundlander and one part English water spaniel. But the black variety of St John's Newfoundlander, which, about Christmas, is landed at Poole, in Dorsetshire, having been almost exclusively fed on fish, finds it hard to adapt to British biscuit.' There are now more yellow Labradors about, sometimes confused with the glorious golden retriever, and their progeny are perhaps the most popular all-round shooting dogs, classed with the Chesapeake as the world's finest swimmers (Frenchmen might vote for the Standard Poodle!), and able to find and retrieve or do virtually everything asked of them – apart from 'pointing'.

The pointer more closely resembles a hound in conformation than any other working dog, the two best known being the English and the German short-haired varieties. Although it is believed that the dog is a cross between a hound and a spaniel, its origins remain obscure, but it is certainly a dog of considerable intelligence and a very acute sense of smell. It is true that the ability to scent game is common to all sporting dogs and that many dogs will 'point' or 'set' if adequately trained, but to the pointer 'it comes naturally', which is all that really matters when we take our tireless companions into the stubble fields or out on the hill.

CONSERVATION

Theodore Roosevelt wrote in 1909: 'Game conservation may be of two kinds. In one the individual landed proprietor, or a group of such individuals, erects and maintains a private game reserve, the game being their property just as much as domestic animals. Such preserves often fill a useful purpose and if managed intelligently with a sense of public spirit and due regard for others, may do much good. But wherever the population is sufficiently advanced in intelligence and character, a far preferable and more democratic way of conserving game is by a system of public preserves, of protected nurseries and breeding grounds, while the law defines conditions under which all alike may shoot the game and the restrictions under which all alike must enjoy the privilege. It is the best way that wild creatures of the forest and the mountain can best and most permanently be preserved.' Roosevelt believed in a policy of conser-

This recent Game Conservancy illustration needs no further explanation

vation by concern; wildlife, he held, was a renewable resource, which, if harvested scientifically, and not faster than the creatures themselves reproduced, might last for ever.

The word 'conservation' had never been heard of in America until that time, and Roosevelt can claim to have started a crusade for the preservation of all wild life threatened by the human conquest of nature, which overnight became, and has remained, the label of an important national issue. In an article published recently in the *Shooting Times and Country Magazine*, a leading member of the British Game Conservancy (an organisation which had grown from the pre-war ICI Game Research Station), pointed out that state-aided wildlife schemes in America were designed to unite farmers, sportsmen and other conservationists in preserving their natural heritage: 'The amount of funding in America is now enviable,' he wrote, 'the enthusiasm by all concerned, infectious, and the harmony and goodwill refreshing.' Game management (written about earlier in the

President Theodore Roosevelt (centre)

book, on page 15) has merely been one way of putting such ideals into practice – conservation, in the broader sense, not always being quite so straightforward.

In Europe, the first deliberate controls on the preservation of wildlife habitat are not known, but it is recorded that William and Mary decreed in 1694 that no likely nesting cover was to be burned in the spring. Systematic heather burning on the Scottish grouse moors in order to improve grouse habitat, however, did not begin until the 1850s. The planting of game cover to facilitate shooting probably started much earlier, but in Hungary the 'remises' mentioned by writers at the beginning of the nineteenth century, normally served two purposes, the second being to encourage game propagation. Over-production of game, however, also has its disadvantages and destructive 'epizootic' (epidemic) diseases will usually be the result. In Great Britain over-grazing and afforestation of the uplands, an excessive use of pesticides with the ploughing up of cover in the lowlands, and indiscriminate drainage of the wetlands, have all contributed to the demise of much of our truly wild game. Unless, therefore, there is an increasing unity of purpose and co-operation towards conservation between sportsmen and their organising bodies, and all who live and work in the countryside, game management and game laws may, in the longer term, become irrelevant.

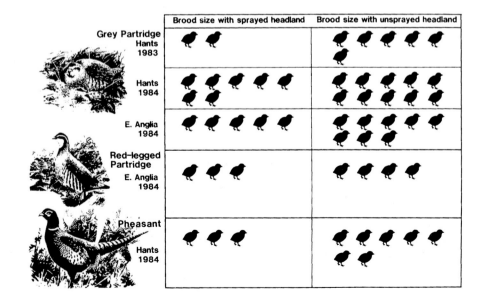

Game killed by the 2nd Marquis of Ripon from 1867 to 1923

Date													Total
1914	2,315	1,628	4,434	6	7	42	–	–	178	709	78		9,467
1915	3,078	2,576	2,595	17	6	5	–	–	341	594	96		9,311
1916	3,435	613	875	8	3	–	–	–	116	474	105		5,629
1917	2,087	1,159	1,990	15	4	9	1	–	168	584	36		6,053
1918	1,445	878	1,279	10	3	4	–	–	128	544	184		4,492
1919	1,097	1,151	1,185	9	–	13	–	–	156	619	262		4,492
1920	765	635	1,527	16	6	14	–	–	144	899	117		4,172
1921	1,984	1,242	2,051	16	7	18	–	–	190	793	82		6,413
1922	992	1,307	2,289	7	4	10	–	–	182	438	134		5,363
1923*	915	356	–	–	2	4	–	–	51	346	200		1,874
1867	18,183	11,595	17,258	106	44	117	1	–	1,654	6,020	1,288		57,266
1913	79,320	112,598	222,976	2,454	2,882	3,452	94	45	30,280	34,118	11,328		499,567
Total	97,503	124,193	241,234	2,560	2,926	3,569	95	45	31,934	40,138	12,616		556,813

*This is only up to 22nd September 1923. On that date Lord Ripon was shooting on Dallowgill Moor near Ripon and killed 165 Grouse and one Snipe. At 3.15 p.m. after a drive in which he had killed 51 Grouse Lord Ripon dropped dead in the heather. He was born 29th January 1852 and was therefore in his 72nd year.

Lord Ripon's Game Book

Four great shooting figures of the Edwardian era: Lord de Grey (on the left); Lord Huntingford (seated); The Maharajah Duleep Singh (standing); and Lord Walsingham (on the right)

Game should not be harvested faster than it reproduces, President Roosevelt had declared. 'Laying stress upon the mere quantity of game killed, and the publication of the record of slaughter, are sure signs of unhealthy decadence in sportsmanship.'

When the sport of 'shooting flying' was introduced in Great Britain during the mid-eighteenth century, large bags of game were at first regarded with a feeling of abhorrence. 'To show the *abundance*, rather than the *exploit* itself', was a sin in the eyes of the Rev William Daniels, author of *Rural Sports*, published in 1812, but he went on to say that 'the real sportsman may feel a twinge whenever he sees a hen pheasant destroyed'. Indeed he suggested that some excesses should be regarded as offences punishable by fines. Not so on the Continent, where at that time it was customary to drive game with as many as a thousand beaters, some stretching out long nets, over shooters, each supported by three loaders armed with seldom less than six shotguns.

There is no doubt that from 1870 to the outbreak of hostilities in 1914 massive bags were also taken in Great Britain. The Marquess of Ripon, formerly Lord de Grey, and the notorious Lord Walsingham, both outstanding shots, were among those who reaped more than their fair share of the spoil. On one occasion, it is told, standing side by side in a hollow in Yorkshire, taking by mutual arrangement alternate birds, they accounted for 98 pheasants with 100 cartridges. It happened that a covey of 8 partridges also flew overhead, each shooter scoring with both guns, so killing the entire covey. Jonathan Ruffer, in his superlative book *The Big Shots*, states that the two men were 'considered men apart as they could shoot so quickly'. He continues 'but even at the turn of the century when shoots were at their prime, Lord de Grey could write, "When I am sitting in a tent taking part in a lengthy luncheon of many courses, served by a host of retainers, my memory carries me back to a time many years ago when we worked harder for our sport, and when seated under a hedge, our mid-day meal consisted of a sandwich – and I am inclined to think that those were better and healthier days. Certainly the young men were keener sportsmen".' Unfortunately those that crave for massive bags today would not necessarily share de Grey's professional opinion.

Commercial shooting, which is a comparatively new angle on a now traditional sport, although providing employment for many people, has many disadvantages – not least the tendency to give game shooting a bad name. Stories of pheasants being buried for want of a market may have been exaggerated, but low reared pheasants or partridges flushed at high volume, or tame duck driven in hundreds off a pond, are shooting practices often criticised today as unnecessary slaughter. Those who take part in such massacres may know no better, but

George Phillipi, one of the finest British shots between the wars, used to place an order with Purdey's for around 25,000 cartridges each season

it is a sad reflection on the organisers and bad publicity for the sporting Gun. Hugh Gladstone, in his book *Record Bags*, last published in the 1930s at a time when large numbers of birds were still being taken, draws a clear distinction between the words 'Sportsman' and 'Shooter'. 'A sportsman would obtain sport by his knowledge of Game, Dogs and Venery in general, whereas many a present day shooter obtains his shooting without any such knowledge.' Much is being done to put matters right, but over half a century later, we may ask ourselves to which of these categories we belong?

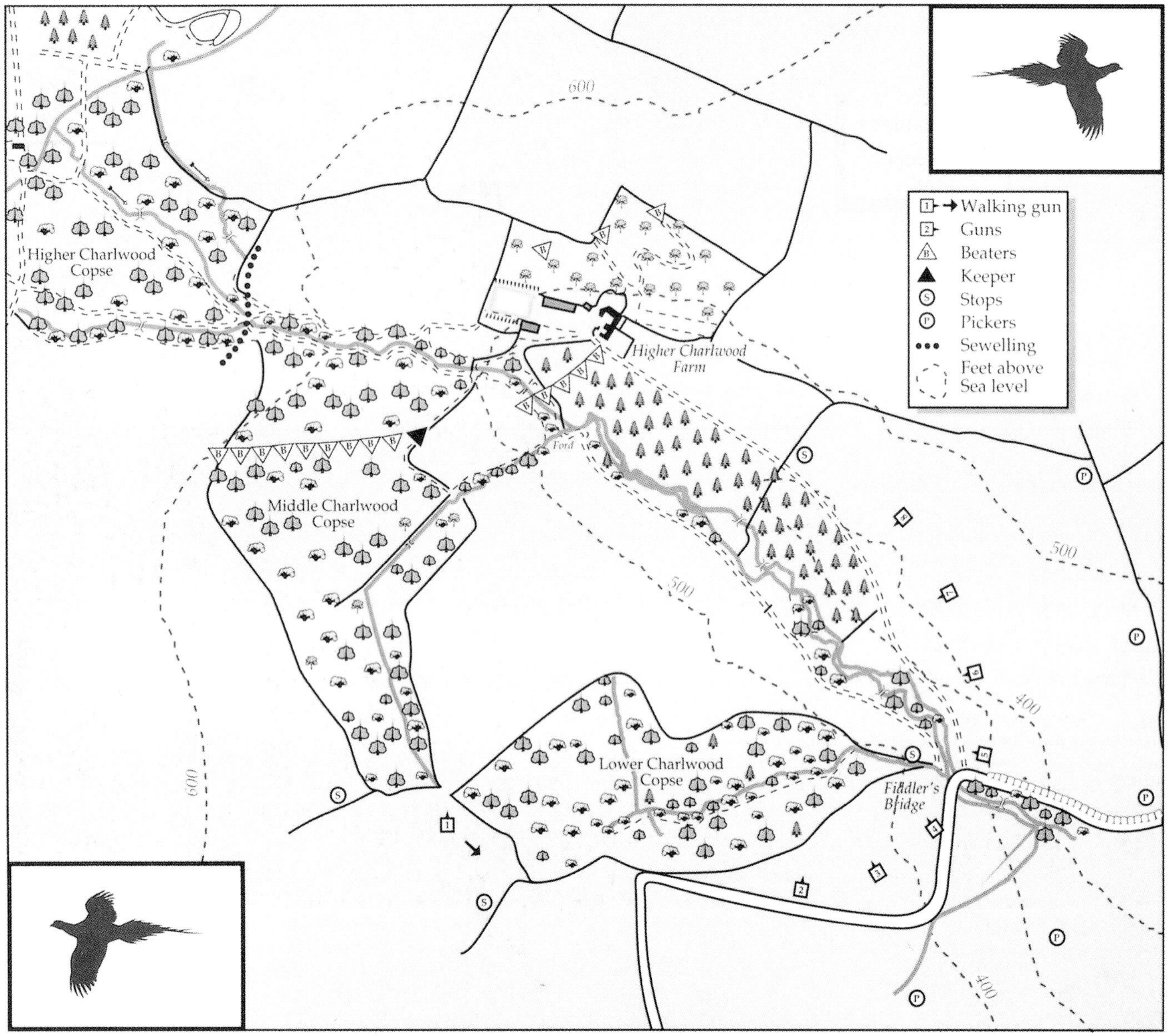

PHEASANT DRIVING

See! from the brake the whirring pheasant springs,
and mounts exulting on triumphant wings.

POPE

Many old sporting prints depict the pheasant complacently awaiting dislodgement by teams of spaniels, in order presumably not to make it too difficult for the leisurely sportsman to shoot him at close range. But pheasants do not have such a predilection for suicide. It is true that dog teams were the forerunners of today's beating line, but they did not go unassisted. Stops were employed, just as they are now, to prevent pheasants legging it to every hedgerow in the parish.

In contrast to modern methods of driving pheasants, and when there were only unhandy weapons available of limited range, the object of the old-time keeper was to present the maximum number of birds as close as possible to the Guns. Once the bird was out of sight it was believed lost for ever, very different to the cardinal principles of modern shooting – that of encouraging birds away from home in order to bring them back again high over the Guns. It has been said that a skilful keeper can drive his pheasants exactly where he wants them; as one famous shot of the Victorian era once boasted, 'I can easily have a covertful driven into my own dining room.'

Fortunately for pheasants most keepers do not find driving them quite so straightforward. First a keeper must consider the time of year; early on in the season there may be too much ground cover, later too little, and many birds will stray away from home. Secondly he must decide how to flush them as good sporting shots. On flat ground he may have pre-arranged flushing points, most likely planted to enhance the shooting, making it necessary to blank in wide areas to collect the birds in the right places. He may also have to surround the area with paper sewelling and stops, and to beat those coverts he least wants to disturb early, and any root crops before the sun leaves them later on. Thirdly he needs a quiet line of beaters, not always with dogs, that he can move from drive to drive with the maximum effect and the minimum of effort.

Map labels

Higher Charlwood Copse

Higher Charlwood Farm

Middle Charlwood Copse

Lower Charlwood Copse

Fiddler's Bridge

Ford

Legend

1 → Walking gun
2 Guns
B Beaters
▲ Keeper
S Stops
P Pickers
••• Sewelling
Feet above Sea level

GROUSE DRIVING

I see against the cloudness blue
the beaters rising into view.
ALFRED COCHRANE

There are about 500 grouse moors in the British Isles
with some 3,000 listed shoots in Scotland alone,
many of which employ full time gamekeepers.
'Grousing' has become so popular with sportsmen
from home and abroad, that shoots now net a
combined total of not far short of £100 million per
season.

Such international business has to be organised
efficiently, and a day of driven grouse is as important
as organising troops on a battlefield. But before battle
can commence there are months of detailed preparation, which, apart from routine conservation, is likely
to include work on long-standing sets of butts.
Sometimes butts are moved to give new sight-lines,
but always they are positioned with the contours and
the direction of alternative beats very much in mind.

The front line troops will normally consist of
fifteen or twenty well drilled and enthusiastic beaters
and several experienced flankers, all properly equip-
ped for bad weather and armed with flags. Behind the
butts are the pickers-up, each with a carefully trained
dog. The keeper must get his forces into position with
the minimum disturbance, starting a drive as much as
a mile back from the eight or nine Guns, once they
are safely in their butts.

On the sound of the keeper's horn the line will
move slowly forward, or in a long half circle around
the hill, with a gap of 10yd (9m) or so between
beaters. The keeper should know the corries and the
gullies like the back of his hand and, by signalling or
using a walkie-talkie, be able to cut off any recognised escape routes by activating his trusted flankers.
The time of day plays a major part in planning the
sequence of each drive and the wind in choosing its
direction. Flags must be waved immediately that a
pack of grouse U-turns, but at other times there is
often need for considerable caution.

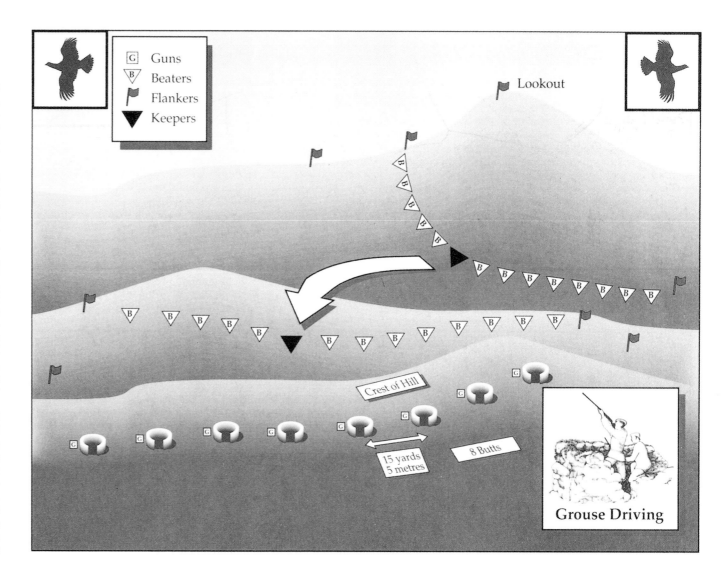

Grouse Driving

PARTRIDGE DRIVING

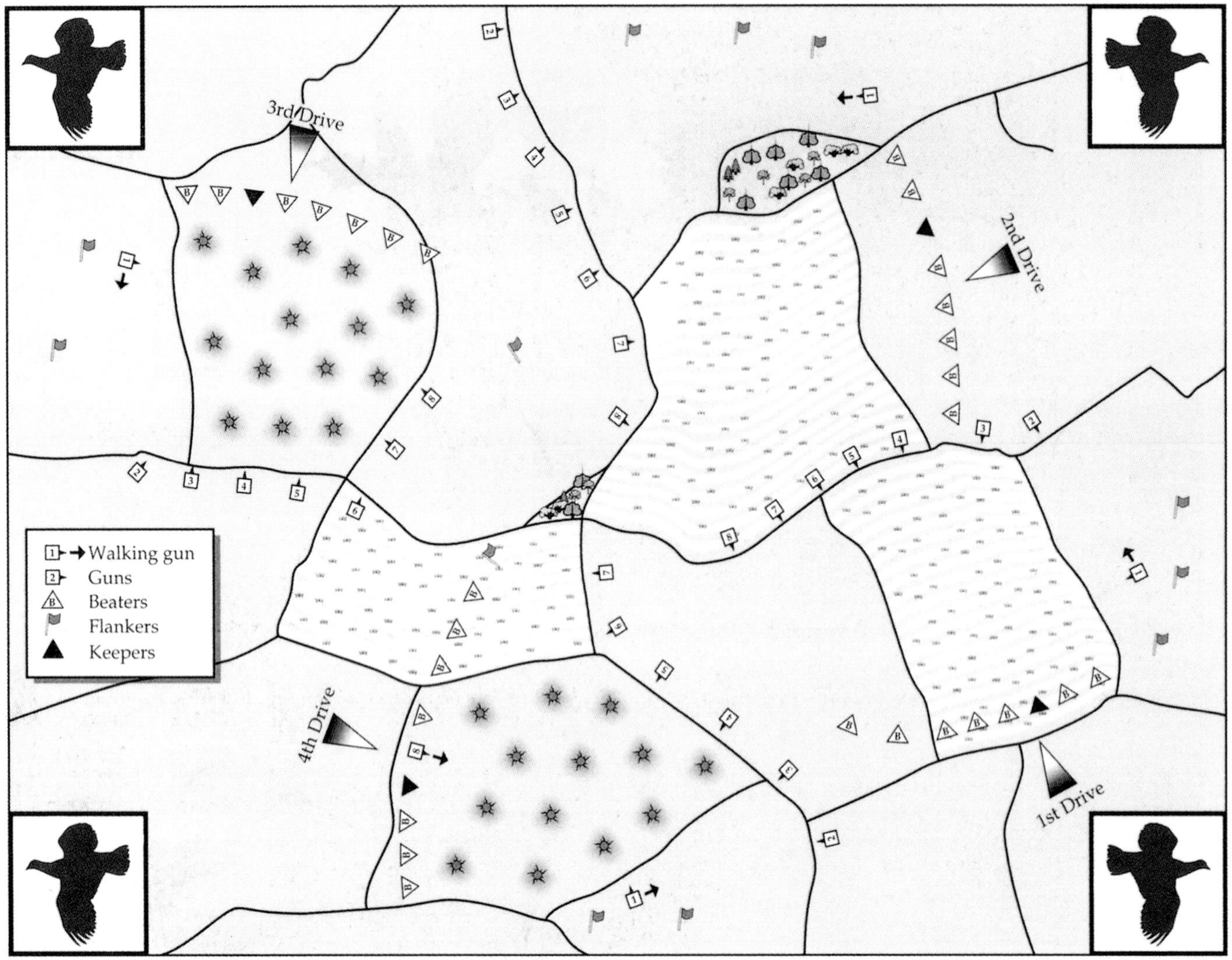

Legend:
- 1 → Walking gun
- 2 Guns
- B Beaters
- Flankers
- ▲ Keepers

(Map labels: 3rd Drive, 2nd Drive, 4th Drive, 1st Drive)

Too little space, the partridge swift as wind,
Quick darts athwart, and bilks her death behind.
BUXTON

Partridges will lie close in foggy weather, their scent being weak for dogs to follow, but when a breeze is blowing they will take to the air with alacrity. At the start of the shooting season coveys may fly only for short distances, often dropping in to the next field when they are disturbed; but towards November they become very wild, and often fly for a mile or more, and at great pace. The keeper's job is to keep the birds within the boundaries of his shoot, and this he will accomplish only with considerable skill and cunning.

The methods of driving partridges were clearly explained by Payne-Gallwey in 1892 and by Alington in 1904, and today they have changed little. Beaters walk in a line carrying white flags, with the outer 'flankers' carrying distinct flags. The beaters, like the birds, are out of sight of the Guns so the centre member, usually the keeper, carries a whistle or horn in order to signal that coveys are flying towards the Guns. The aim is to drive the birds as high as possible to give testing shots – usually by using shelter belts, tall hedges or, if possible, by placing the Guns along the bottom of a valley. Driving is made easier if root crops are available, in which case the flanked coveys are first encouraged into the holding cover before being driven in the right direction.

Direction is all important, not that many partridge are wont to follow instructions. It is possible by careful planning to drive partridge in rotation so that birds are not pushed too far from the territory they have made their own. It is also necessary that the line of Guns is well concealed, for it is practical to take aim effectively at only a small proportion of the birds driven.

MIGRATION

Some think to northern coasts their flight tend,
or to the moon in midnight hours ascend.

JOHN GAY

Fortunately there are still a few mysteries left in life and the migration of birds continues to fascinate us. Among the most remarkable travellers are Arctic terns, which migrate to the Antarctic, literally between the ends of the earth, but others, including some varieties of game birds, have habits that are equally astonishing.

Using sophisticated radar, migrants have been tracked through every part of the globe. Geese flying south from Nova Scotia have been followed to heights of 6,500ft (2,000m) over Bermuda, rising to 21,000ft (6,500m) over Antigua before making a gradual descent to the South American mainland – a nonstop flight of more than 3,000 miles (4,800km) accomplished in less than 90 hours at an average speed of around 35mph (55kmph). Analysis of compass headings has shown that after leaving North America the birds invariably fly steadily southeast until they reach Bermuda where they must then turn southwest or be swept out to sea by the prevailing winds. Such accurate navigation, it is now believed, is not only the result of the earth's magnetic field, but, like our own technique, is also dependent on the sun and the stars. Shorter flights are usually made by night.

The European woodcock, unknown to many who shoot them, migrates across England's eastern seaboard at specific times of the year. The Rev William Daniels, writing in 1801, said that 'the time of their appearance in Sweden coincides exactly with that of their departure from Great Britain.' He continues, 'Sportsmen on the coast, however, know not the time of this departure . . . if the wind be propitious, the cock are gone immediately, if not, they will wait in the neighbouring woods, in the ling or the furze, until legitimately or otherwise, the local folk have a bonanza and the whole countryside echoes with the discharge of guns. Then, where hundreds have been seen one day, there will not be a single bird the next.'

Migrating birds have always fallen prey to so called sportsmen, particularly in Mediterranean countries, and, sadly, the problem is not getting any better.

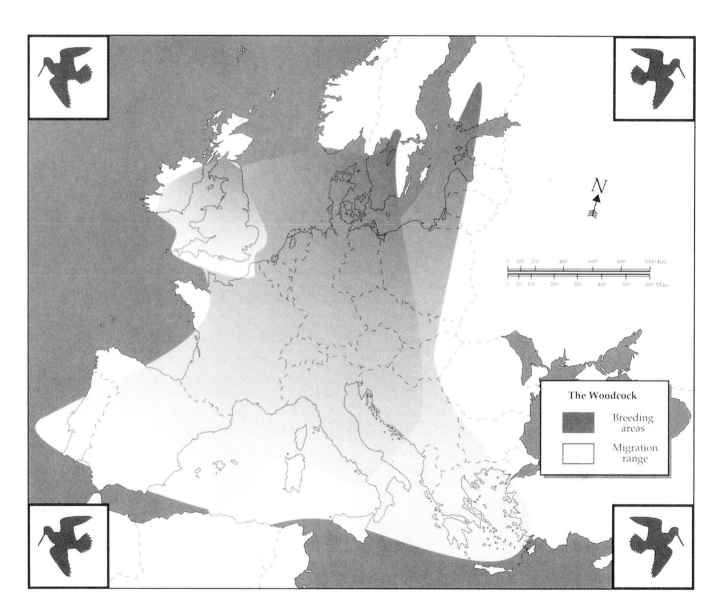

N

The Woodcock

Breeding areas

Migration range

89

THE FUTURE

*Better, by far, to mix flint and steel – the odd
spark may enliven proceedings.*

Writing about today's English syndicate shoot, John
Marchington in his *Field Bedside Book*, published in
1967, said that 'to select eight men for a syndicate
who completely blend in is almost impossible but,
even if it were not, the result might well be dull
company.' In Great Britain most shoots now revolve

'When my bloke kills another – he'll have shot one!'

The only birds left to retrieve may be those that drop dead from
old age!

round the 'syndicate', each member contributing to
the *bonhomie* – and the kitty! An increasing number
of days may well be let to 'foreigners', as may happen
on those few shoots having no syndicate; but strictly
private shoots, which let no days to outsiders, are few
and far between. The shooting field, in any part of
the world, is no place for dull company, and today's
dwindling experience of 'man against nature' is a
privilege for everyone to share. But once a shoot has
embarked on the commercial trail there is no turning
back, and flint and steel may well take on another
meaning.

The demand for most kinds of British field sport
continues to be staggering. The pheasant shooting in
Eastern Europe is much sought after, as is the
partridge shooting in Spain, but apart from in
America, where there is little or no driven game
(pheasant are driven on Long Island), the greatest
variety of organised shooting is available principally
in the British Isles. Such notoriety leads sadly to abuse
– and a look into the future will hardly go amiss.

The continuing decline in farm incomes has forced
farmers to look increasingly for other profitable
enterprises. As shooting provides a feasible alternative – one with which they may already be familiar,
and which does not harm their land – the opportunity
of making a quick 'buck' from farming game birds
grows steadily more attractive, and with it the
motivation for overstocking and other unpleasant
practices. Just as syndicate shooting took off during
the sixties, let days in the seventies and corporate
days (a way of entertaining business colleagues) in the
eighties, it is likely that pay days on 'game farms' will
take off during the nineties. New marketing techniques will see that more 'lead-free' farmed birds
reach the shops, while surplus pheasant, partridge
or duck will be driven over any undiscerning Tom,
Dick or Harry who has sufficient funds to shoot
them. In order to prevent this happening lead
poisoning, already a major environmental issue, must
be tackled fast, and a satisfactory alternative to lead
shot developed (steel shot, now mandatory in most
American States, ruins the barrels of most shotguns
and is ballistically inferior).

Fortunately, many sporting Guns now recognise
the need to 'get their house in order' before there is
any concerted government intervention and various
'codes of practice' have been introduced, spelling out
revised sporting guidelines. Hopefully, shoot owners
who ignore such measures will soon discover that
they themselves are ignored, and game birds will
continue to enjoy the same privileges that have so
long been denied their domestic counterparts. Game
bird shooting has become a major industry, employing a growing number of people, and landowners,
shoot organisers, gamekeepers and cartridge manufacturers will all bear an increasing responsibility to
see that the sport continues to prosper.

Fact or fantasy? The idea of shooting infra-red beams at birds
fitted with light-reflecting collars is already technically possible.
The birds may grow old – but increasingly cunning, and
shooting at them becomes a challenging competition. (Only the
dogs get bored!)

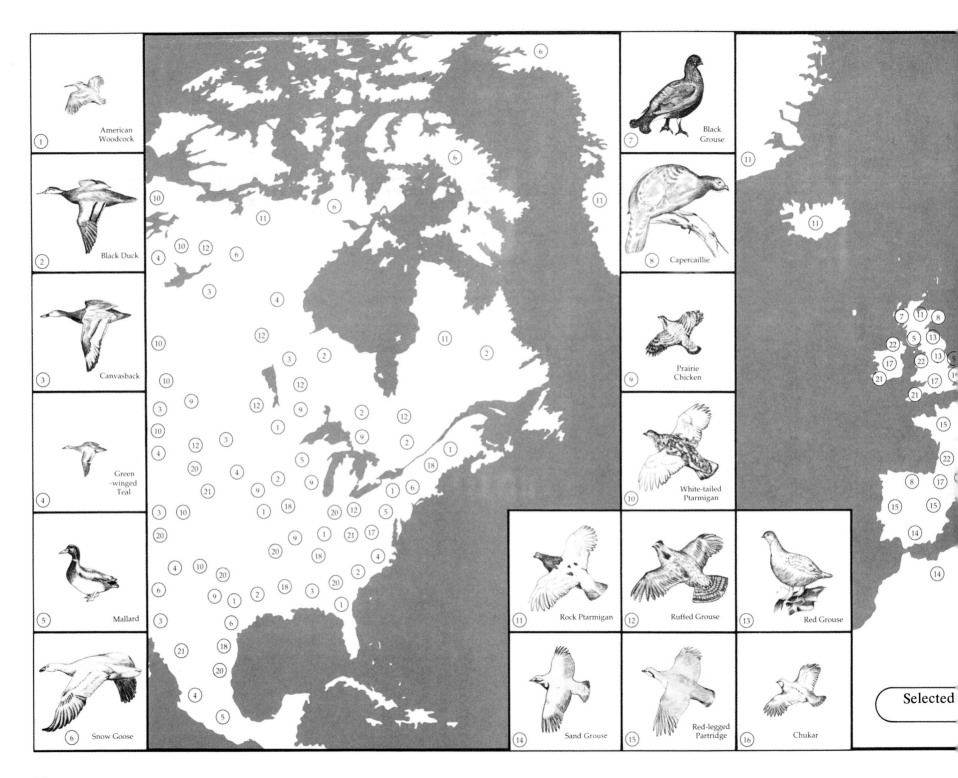

American Woodcock ①
Black Duck ②
Canvasback ③
Green -winged Teal ④
Mallard ⑤
Snow Goose ⑥

Black Grouse ⑦
Capercaillie ⑧
Prairie Chicken ⑨
White-tailed Ptarmigan ⑩
Rock Ptarmigan ⑪
Ruffed Grouse ⑫
Red Grouse ⑬
Sand Grouse ⑭
Red-legged Partridge ⑮
Chukar ⑯

Selected

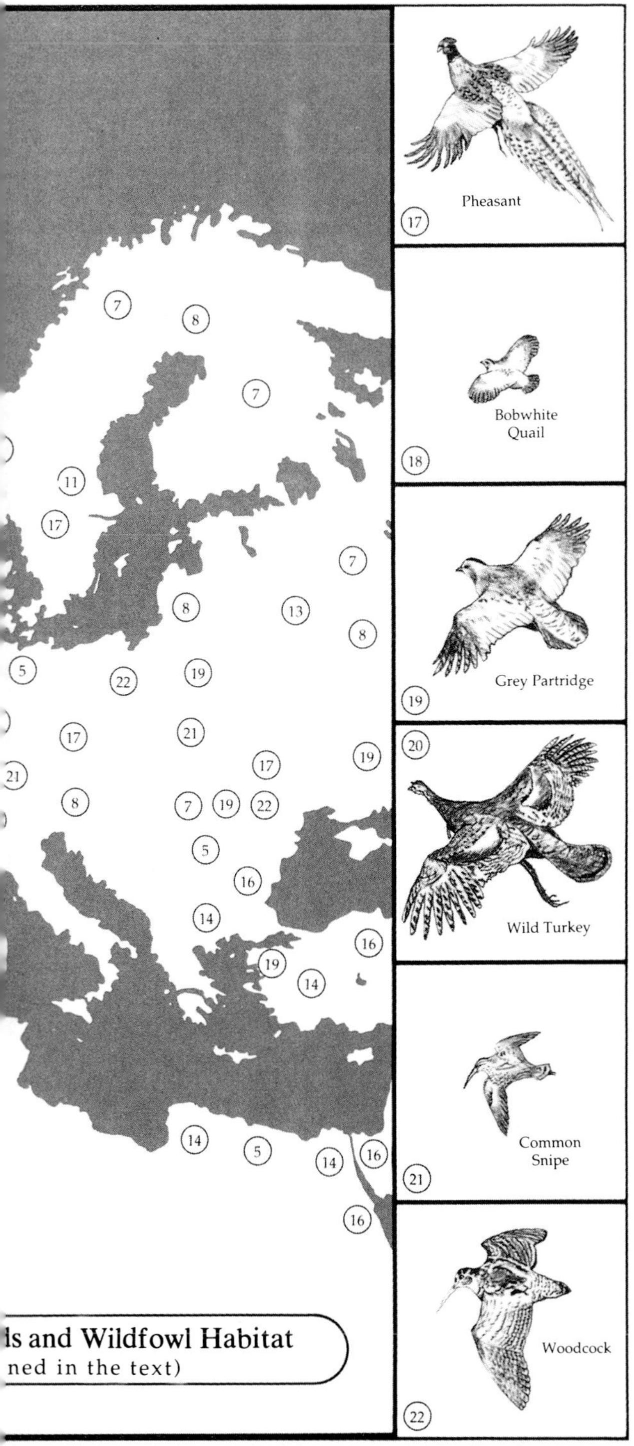
Pheasant
Bobwhite Quail
Grey Partridge
Wild Turkey
Common Snipe
Woodcock
ls and Wildfowl Habitat
ned in the text)

LIST OF PAINTINGS

Paintings by Andrew Ellis reproduced in this book

Page			
17	Boy shooting rabbits	Oil	30 × 40in
19	Rough shooting	Watercolour	16 × 22in
21	Walking up pheasants	Watercolour	16 × 22in
23	Pheasant 'sitting it out'	Watercolour	16 × 22in
25	'Left and right'	Watercolour	22 × 16in
26	Walking up grouse	Watercolour	16 × 22in
29	'Bombing the butts'	Watercolour	16 × 22in
31	'Love at the lek'	Watercolour	16 × 22in
33	'Playing hard to get'	Watercolour	16 × 22in
35	Ruffed grouse	Watercolour	16 × 22in
36–7	Sandgrouse	Watercolour	14 × 28in
39	Quail	Watercolour	16 × 22in
40–1	Prairie chicken	Watercolour	16 × 28in
43	Walking up partridge	Watercolour	16 × 22in
45	'First partridge drive'	Watercolour	16 × 22in
46	Spanish partridge shooting	Watercolour	16 × 22in
49	'The mating call'	Watercolour	16 × 22in
51	Wild turkey shoot	Watercolour	16 × 22in
53	Barnacle geese	Watercolour	14 × 28in
55	Snow geese	Watercolour	16 × 22in
56–7	Pintail duck in India	Oil	24 × 36in
58	'The evening flight'	Watercolour	22 × 16in
60–1	Punt gunning	Watercolour	16 × 28in
63	'The timorous teal'	Watercolour	22 × 16in
65	Canvas-back in winter	Watercolour	16 × 22in
67	Black duck in Australia	Watercolour	16 × 22in
69	'Dodging the sunbeams'	Watercolour	16 × 22in
71	The American woodcock	Watercolour	16 × 22in
73	'The elusive snipe'	Watercolour	16 × 22in
74	Pigeon shoot	Watercolour	22 × 16in
75	Rock pigeon	Watercolour	16 × 22in
76	Hen harriers	Watercolour	16 × 22in
78	The poachers	Watercolour	16 × 22in

Enquiries about the originals, or about reproductions, may be made to:
Andrew Ellis, Ashcombe Tower, Dawlish, Devon, EX7 0PY, England.

TERMINOLOGY

Collective terms for British sporting birds of the eighteenth century. Many (marked with an asterisk) are still in use today.

*Covey of partridge
Nide of pheasants (commonly called a *ni* or *nye*)
*Pack of grouse
*Wisp or walk of snipe(s)
Wing or congregation of plovers
*Flock of geese
*Gaggle of geese (on water)
*Skein of geese (on wing)
*Company of widgeon
*Spring of teal
Dopping of sheldrakes
Covert of coots
*Herd of curlews
Sedge of herons
*Bevy of quail(s)
*Flight of woodcock(s)
Trip of dottrell
Team of ducks (on wing)
Paddling of ducks (on water)
Sord or suit of mallards
Flock of bustards
Trip or bunch of wildfowl (small number)

The (s) has been dropped.

ENGLISH
OPEN SEASONS

Common snipe	12 August	– 31 January
Grouse	12 August	– 10 December
Black game	20 August	– 10 December
Geese *Inland*	1 September	– 31 January
Wild duck *Foreshore*	1 September	– 20 February
Partridge	1 September	– 1 February
Woodcock	1 October	– 31 January
Pheasant	1 October	– 1 February

SCOTTISH
OPEN SEASONS

Grouse	12 August	– 10 December
Ptarmigan	12 August	– 10 December
Woodcock	1 September	– 31 January
Capercaillie	1 October	– 31 January

EUROPEAN
OPEN SEASONS

eg for woodcock

Sweden	21 August	– 31 December
Norway	21 August	– 1 March
Italy	28 August	– 31 March
Belgium	1 September	– 31 March
W Germany	1 September	– 5 April
France	4 September	– 6 January
Spain	11 September	– 1 March
Holland	1 October	– 31 January

AMERICAN
OPEN SEASONS

These vary between the individual states.

ACKNOWLEDGEMENTS

I would like to thank all those who have helped me with this fourth sporting story, in particular Charles Coles, whose detailed knowledge of game birds and the shooting scene was of immense value. The Duke of Wellington, an experienced shoot owner, and an authority on Spain, sporting guns and gun dogs, was extremely generous to have taken such trouble with the foreword. I am also grateful to Don Haas, an avid quail hunter and wildfowler, who from his home in California helped me with much of the information on hunting game birds and wildfowl in America. Ethan Danielson, also from America, has again produced some outstanding line drawings, which I appreciate greatly, and I am also indebted to Sue Hall and Mike Head for compiling this book so successfully. I have had the assistance of many willing librarians in many parts of the world, but I should like to mention the British Library, and the kindness of Hugh Lowry and John Conroy, who may have found me a more difficult author to deal with than most!

My series of sporting books would never have been possible without the cheerful co-operation of the talented young artists I have commissioned to illustrate them. Andrew Ellis started working on the first plates for this book when he was aged only 16 and still at college, and it is to his great credit that he has completed so many superb and varied paintings and drawings within such a strict three-year timetable. Now turning his attention, for a while, to fishing, he is a sporting artist with a very bright future indeed. Andrew has spent many hours painting in my studio, which overlooks the glorious Devon countryside, and my thanks would not be complete if I did not mention my wife, Annette, an accomplished artist herself, who deserved several Brownie points for clearing up the paint and feathers after him!